ADVANCE PRAISE FOR

THE ENTREPRENEUR'S TRAP

There are only a few people in the world who can do what Tina does, making all that "behind the scenes" stuff make sense, and in Tina's case, she even makes it simple AND fun. This book is a practical and useful guide for entrepreneurs who are ready to dig deep under the surface, and let go of the heartache of working way too hard for their businesses."

Andrea J.Lee, Founder and CEO, WealthyThoughtLeader.com

"In the 10 years of running Box of Crayons we've hit three income plateaus where I've been working my butt off and I've been certain it's IMPOSSIBLE to do more. And each time I've managed to automate part of the business—and our income (and my free time) has increased again. We're at another plateau right now. And Tina's book is one of the tools I'm using to find out how to make the next leap."

Michael Bungay Stanier, Senior Partner, Box of Crayons & author of 'Do More Great Work'

"Tina has a willingness to do what is a challenge for so many – to let go of what could stop her and do whatever it takes to create the business she wants. This book is a reflection of that and lays out a simple path to help you do the same with finesse and her trademark "get it done fast" style."

David Neagle, Author of *The Millions Within* & Master Income Acceleration Coach

"Simply put, Tina is the best of class. With her years of experience she knows more about how to run and grow an online business than most business owners. And, more importantly, she has the utmost integrity. She does what she says she's going to do, and then some."

Michael Port, NY Times bestselling author of *Book Yourself Solid*, MichaelPort.com

"This book is the answer to a woman entrepreneur's prayers! Tina has taken all of the most important decisions you need to consider—both big and small—to make your business flow smoothly and condensed them into a simple set of systems that are easy to follow. I can't imagine growing a business today without the wealth of Tina's insights, exercises and wisdom shared in this book, on how to make any business—including yours—fabulous, fun and joyful to run."

Kendall SummerHawk , Leading Expert in Women Entrepreneurs and Money, Co-founder of the International Association of Women in Business Coaching

"This book is a must-read for any business owner just starting out on their own entrepreneur journey. I wish I'd had this book when I started my business, and saved myself the time and hassle of putting the wrong systems in place. Tina's simple steps and clear language really do take the mystery out of setting up an online business."

Suzanne Evans, Suzanne Evans Coaching LLC

"Following Tina's advice, in a few short months I was able to build systems into my business which pulled me out of the middle and opened up my time to focus on the work I should be doing, including a rebranding of my business. Thank you Tina, with your help I have moved from being self-employed to owning a legacy business. You helped me see the light and I am sure you will help so many others with this wonderful new book!"

Donna Cravotta, Social Sage PR

"*The Entrepreneur's Trap* is a must-read for the business owner who wants a sustainable business AND a sustainable life. *Focus on the intersection of what you love and what serves the business. Build the structure you want and not just what everyone else is doing. Plan for 3 steps ahead, not 3 years.* There are so many good lessons in this book!"

Caroline Ceniza-Levine, SixFigureStart.com

"If you have a business or are considering starting a business you need this book...it's a must read as it not only lays the foundation of a lot of things you won't think about before you start your business but it will make you more aware of the areas you really need to concentrate on to leverage your existing business as well. This should be a must read for every business owner. I sure wish I had it 15 years ago when I started my business."

Diane Conklin, Founder of CompleteMarketingSystems.com

"For those of you who have decided that 'good enough' just is NOT 'good enough' any more – this is the book for you! Tina Forsyth really cares about you... on every page, she cheers you on with stories from her own experience and provides you with the tools and techniques to get you from good to great. No matter where you are in your business, you can benefit from the easy-to-apply information in this book. So do it now! You and your loved ones will be happy you did."

Pat Mussieux, Founder, WealthyWomenLeaders.com

"Put on your big girl panties and get ready for a big reality check from Tina Forsyth! You're going to see yourself and how you run your business as soon as you open the pages: from the blissful denial of a newbie to "OMG, something's gotta change" a few years into it. But Tina's not here to point out your weak spots and leave you high and dry. She delivers solutions that ANY business owner can put into place no matter how new or how seasoned you are. If your business is starting to feel more like a JOB and less like the dream you envisioned, pick up this book and do exactly what Tina says."

Nancy Marmolejo, VivaVisibility.com

"With all the options available to entrepreneurs these days it is really easy to get caught up in the trap of "doing it because everyone else is" and finding yourself with a business that you don't really want. Tina's book is a roadmap to avoiding that trap and creating a business that gives you the space and freedom to enjoy everything else that is important to you."

Milana Leshinsky, Author of "Recurring Revenue Business Blueprint," Milana.com

"This book is such a reflection of what I love about Tina. It is real, straight, deeply insightful, and highly practical as well. Tina is a master at bringing the truth to the forefront and using it to help people create more freedom. The material within is invaluable if you are committed to those things and want to take stock of your business and make it work for you."

Darla LeDoux, Profit Acceleration Coach, AlignandProfit.com

"Tina Forsyth is a very rare person. She tells it like it is – giving you the tools to succeed as an entrepreneur in business. I have learned more from Tina about how to be a successful Entrepreneur in a few months than I did attending graduate school to obtain an MBA."

Marie A. O'Neill, CEO Padma Life Coaching

"Tina, you've done it again! What I love about this book is that this is simply one more example of how you are always creating content that meets the business owner exactly where they are as an entrepreneur. In your work you are consistently opening doors to show entrepreneurs that achieving their dream of business success is obtainable and they may be working too darn hard to get there."

Brenda Violette, Violette Business Services, LLC, BrendaViolette.com

"Tina is quite simply the best when it comes to supporting entrepreneurs run their business in a way that works (ie not running yourself into the ground!) This book outlines exactly how to do that—and is brilliantly written in Tina's fun, 'tell it how it is' style. Full of invaluable tips and advice, this book is a MUST READ for any business owner—no matter what stage of business you are at. It will save you time, energy and money— and quite possibly your sanity! Tina knows what she is talking about—and what she is talking about works."

Kate Gerry, Systems and Team Expert. Certified Online Business Manager, OnlineBusinessManager.uk.com

"If I had this book when I started my business I would have saved countless hours and thousands of dollars that I basically threw out the window! This book is a must read for all entrepreneurs who want to create organizational systems that truly allow them to find freedom in their business! I feel like a weight has been lifted off my shoulders, my team is capable of handling projects with ease and I am able to focus on growth and generating revenue!"

Emily Holdridge, Co-founder & CEO of Everything Happy

"Having experienced much of what Tina covers in this book, I only wish she had written it when I started out as an entrepreneur in 2001. What Tina delves into is truly a case of 'you don't know what you don't know', but now with The Entrepreneur's Trap, you can avoid falling into the Trap (or get out of it) and create the successful business you love without having to sacrifice what's most important to you. I'm making The Entrepreneur's Trap required reading for all my clients!"

Alicia Forest, MBA, AliciaForest.com

"Everyone wants a business that runs itself—or at least as close to that ideal as possible! But it's not like you were born with the ability to set up systems, the right team, and putting all the pieces together to create a business that truly supports you and your lifestyle. Tina truly understands where entrepreneurs live. She knows what you want, where you are now, and where you want to be. This book will give you the clearest path to getting there in the shortest amount of time.

Elizabeth Purvis, GoddessBusinessSchool.com

"Who in their right mind goes into business for themselves because they like the boring management of the business, right? I sure didn't, but because of my own business ignorance, I nearly went broke from my first business, my plastic surgery practice. In *The Entrepreneur's Trap*, Tina lays out the principles and best practices of efficient entrepreneurship, things I ended up learning the hard way. If you read *The Entrepreneur's Trap* and apply what you learn, you'll avoid the trap of having your business run your life."

George C. Huang, M.D., Chief Freedom Officer, Freedompreneur.com

"Tina Forsyth has done it again with *The Entrepreneur's Trap*! She has figured out how to escape the entrepreneur's trap of overwhelm and invested years of her own time in fine-tuning her systems so you don't have to. Why try to figure it how to automate and streamline your business by reinventing the wheel when she has already mastered it? I consider this required reading for any entrepreneur who wants to build a business with a solid foundation for growth and unlimited success."

Fabienne Fredrickson, Client Attraction Mentor, ClientAttraction.com

How to Stop Working Too Much,
Take Back Your Time, & Enjoy Life !

THE ENTREPRENEUR'S TRAP

TINA FORSYTH

Love Your Life

Love Your Life Publishing
St. Peters, MO 63346
www.loveyourlifepublishing.com

ISBN: 978-1-934509-62-3
Library of Congress Control Number: 2012947500
Printed in the United States of America
First Printing 2012

Editing by Gwen Hoffnagle
Cover Design: Cynaotype.ca
Interior Formatting: Indie Designz

Table of Contents

DEDICATION

To my girls, Sam and Lexi–If I can teach you that you can have your freedom while doing what you love, then I know I've done my job well.

—

THE ENTREPRENEUR'S TRAP

INTRODUCTION

When I graduated from high school I decided to get a business degree for the simple fact that I didn't know what else I wanted to do. I knew I wanted to go to college and figured a business degree would be a good default major.

Flash forward to today and I'm happy that I did, as I'm now able to take what I learned in getting a Bachelor of Science in Business Operations and combine that with my twelve-plus years' experience as an entrepreneur, and I get to share with people like you.

I don't believe it's necessary to have a business degree or an MBA to be an entrepreneur, as most of those programs teach you more about how to work for a corporation than they do about running your own business. But I do believe it's necessary to know how to run a business and build it on a strong foundation. Yet many entrepreneurs find this stuff boring; some even want to run screaming from it.

Running the business isn't the fun and sexy side of entrepreneurship, but it is essential to your success and sanity.

Having worked online since 1999, I've had the pleasure (and many times the headache) of learning what it takes to grow a successful business. I spent over seven years working as an Online Business Manager for my clients, running the day-to-day operations for many six—and seven—figure businesses. Being the right-hand gal to these amazing entrepreneurs taught me more than I ever could have learned on my own.

I've spent the past four years teaching our Certified Online Business Manager™ training and working directly with other successful entrepreneurs to get the right systems, teams, and leveraged revenue streams in place to run their businesses. There is nothing I love more than seeing an entrepreneur breathe a sigh of relief because they (finally!) have the right foundation in place to grow their business.

My intent with this book is to make it as simple as possible to help you set up a business that can run without you—to help you choose the right business model, the right systems, and the right team to create a business that thrives and doesn't suck up all your time and energy.

And I promise it won't be painful.

So let's have some fun, shall we?

CHAPTER 1
BEWARE OF THE TRAP

How Much Do You Really Need to Work in order to Be Successful?

This is the question that drove me to write this book. In other words, do you have to work your buns off 24/7 to achieve the level of success that you want in your business? Is it necessary to sacrifice your time, energy, and family to be successful? Or can you have it all and work fewer (or reasonable) hours?

You see, I never thought I would be an entrepreneur. And I think this is true for many entrepreneurs in this day and age.

The ease of entry into entrepreneurship and business ownership has drastically shifted in the past ten to fifteen years. It used to be that if you wanted to start a business, it

1

was a process that took many months, if not years. You would start with market research, then create a business plan, find financing and a location (as the world of working from home didn't really exist yet), maybe an employee or two, and then you were able to officially open a business.

Now we live in a world in which someone can have a business idea and literally start their business that same day. Which seems awesome, right?

On one hand it is—I simply LOVE the fact that anyone who wants to take control of their livelihood, do meaningful work, and make more money while enjoying more freedom can do so. But the reality of entrepreneurship is a rude awakening for many people. It's not as simple as: have an idea, get the word out there, get clients, and BAM!—the money comes pouring in while you take an extended lunch in the middle of the day because you don't have a boss looking over your shoulder.

In fact, for many entrepreneurs I know it's the exact opposite. They run into what I call *The Entrepreneur's Trap*.

The Entrepreneur's Trap is when the time, money, and effort that you are putting into your business is not worth the return you are getting.

- Instead of escaping from a boss telling you what to do, you now find your time is dictated by your clients, your team, and other responsibilities of your business.
- Instead of making more money, you are actually making less money simply because it costs so much to make your business run.
- Instead of doing work that you love to do, you find yourself spending most of your day doing things that you hate—but they fall onto your plate as the business owner.

2

This is the "dark side" of entrepreneurship, and it's something that many people don't anticipate until they are knee-deep in it. Put simply, this sucks. And it makes me really sad when I see entrepreneurs suffering like this.

I believe there are two reasons why people fall into this trap:

Reason #1: Your Expectations

There are two extreme views when it comes to entrepreneurial success:

1. The Sacrifice-Your-Life Approach

"You have to be willing to do whatever it takes to succeed and work as hard as you possibly can, even if that means making major sacrifices in other areas of life (time, health, family, etc.)." This is the most visible and most often glamorized version of entrepreneurship—what we read about in magazines and see in movies.

In this case the entrepreneur is so consumed by their business and so dedicated to its success that they take it to the extreme in order to succeed. They will work three days straight without rest, invest their entire life savings, sleep at the office, and never see their kids. They will work ninety hours a week, including weekends, and never take a vacation. Their phone is always on and the ping of a new email wakes them up in the middle of the night to respond. They are exhausted, haggard, and might even have health issues – even dangerously close to full-on burnout. Their relationships are suffering, with a spouse who feels neglected and kids they rarely see (or who only get to see the back of their head lit by a computer screen while they are continually working).

3

But they are willing to sacrifice everything in pursuit of success—to reach that holy grail of success – which sometimes they aren't even clear on. They just know that once they get there, it will all have been worth it, right?

2. The Sit-On-the-Bench-and-Watch-the-Money-Roll-In Approach

The other side of this coin is what I like to call the *passive revenue myth*. This is the dream of creating a business that requires so little of your time and energy that you can essentially work just a few hours a week and make money hand over fist. There are many programs and gurus out there who will sell you this dream and tell you that building a business is just that easy. I'm here to tell you it's not.

Regardless of the type of business you have, you will need to put in time, energy, and effort to make it successful (in other words to make money).Just to be clear, this does not mean you have to work 24/7. But you can't expect to just sit back and watch the money pour in. Even people who live the dream of a four-hour workweek generally had to work pretty hard to get to that point – it didn't happen overnight or as a result of a business-in-a-box that they purchased.

I believe the best answer for most of us lies somewhere in the middle, and that we each need to ask ourselves:

How can I work the least amount possible (time, energy, and effort) to get my desired level of success?

First decide what kind of success you want to create, and then decide how much time, energy, and effort you are willing to put into achieving it. The answer will be different for each person, and we are going to explore this in depth throughout this book.

Reason #2: Not Understanding What It Takes to Run a Business

Picture this... you are making money, sales are higher than ever, and the clients are rolling in. Everything you have been working towards is finally coming true. Woo hoo!

But, to your surprise, it is beginning to feel like your business is sucking the life out of you. Strange things are starting to happen in your business that are causing you alarm:

- Instead of working less, you are now **working 24/7 trying to get everything done, there is no light at the end of the tunnel,** and you have no idea how you got yourself into this mess.
- You have those middle-of-the-night moments, waking up in a cold sweat thinking, **"OMG, did X get done? Yikes! I don't think it did..."**
- **A client complains that you didn't fulfill on a commitment and they want a refund.** You thought everything was great and you aren't sure what went wrong.
- You realize that a team member didn't do something that you emailed them about a few days ago, **and now YOU have to scramble to get it done on time.**
- You feel like you don't know what everyone on your team is working on, and **wonder if stuff is getting done at all**.

5

- **You are tired of everyone bugging you all the time with questions**—why can't they just do their work and leave you alone?
- Because so many to-dos keep coming up at the last minute, **your team is starting to get seriously frustrated with a seemingly constant flow of "Urgent, need this now!" requests,** and they are threatening to leave.
- Your assistant is the only one who knows "how things are done around here," and **you feel trapped and worried that if she leaves, what happens then?**
- You have a certain way that you want things to be done, but it seems like **every time someone else on your team works on it, they do it wrong or miss key pieces**.
- **Your calendar is out of control.** You have no more time to book anything, have missed calls, and have even been double-booked a few times (which never used to happen!).
- **You aren't sure where the money is**, and have no way of knowing if payments are coming in on time (or not!).
- You fly by the seat of your pants, not sure what you are going to offer next and **suffering from the roller-coaster ride of last-minute launches**.
- There is so much work to be done—simple things like replying to emails—**that you never get to the important things that could grow your business.**
- Sadly, **your spouse and/or kids are asking you why you are working so much,** and may **even be begging you to turn off the computer for once so they can spend time with you**.
- You wake up in the morning dreading the day. **What once felt like a lot of fun is now a drag.**

The bottom line is that you are tired, frustrated, and starting to wonder what the heck you've gotten yourself into. It's one thing to GROW a business, but it's another thing to RUN a business—which is what many of us are unprepared for.

This is what I call the *Leaky Bucket Syndrome*. We focus so much on getting more into the bucket (sales, marketing, and clients), but neglect to make sure that the bucket (behind the scenes of your biz) is whole and healthy.

Because it is so easy to get into business these days, many people do so without knowing what it takes to run a business—all that behind-the-scenes stuff that many entrepreneurs find boring, confusing, or downright scary. And yet your behind-the-scenes business operations are ESSENTIAL to your success, and if you don't put the right structure in place in your business, it will cause all kind of chaos and headaches, and can end up costing you a lot of money.

The good news is this: ALL of these things can be solved with the right systems and team in place, which is what the second part of this book is all about. You are in the growing-pains stage, and, with a bit of purposeful work and perseverance, this, too, shall pass (even if it doesn't feel like it right now).

Why this book?

My goals for you are simple:

- to define what success is for you in your business (versus what someone told you it should be)

- to decide what you are willing to invest in time, energy, and money, based on your lifestyle, to achieve this level of success
- to help you get simple and effective systems in place, and the team to support them, so that you don't have it all on your shoulders

Ultimately these are all choices. It is totally up to you how you want to create success in your business (and likewise in your life).

When I was first writing this book I was going to take a really firm stand on certain things and essentially say to you, "This is the way you need to do it all," based on how I run my business. But then I realized that even though my way is right for me, it isn't necessarily the right way for everyone else.

There are no right or wrong choices, as long as you end up with a business that makes you good money and serves what you really want out of your life (vs. sucking the life out of you and your family).

I've written this book to help you find clarity about your business and the various choices you will be faced with on your growth path so that you can decide what success looks like for YOU and set up your business to support that.

There are stories and examples sprinkled throughout, both from my own personal journey as an entrepreneur and from various people that were happy to have me pick their brain while I was writing this book, some of whom are in The Trap and others who have very successfully escaped it or avoided it from day one.

I'm happily into the multiple six-figure range with my business, and have been since 2009. I've shifted my business model from a one-to-one service professional with no team to a training and consulting company with three full-timers and a bunch of part-time/project folks, all of whom work in their own home offices. I've always said that my business is a grand experiment, and that we are happy to be guinea pigs in sharing what we've gone through and learned along the way.

That being said, I certainly don't consider myself to be at the pinnacle of success. I'm not a seven- or eight-figure business owner who "has it all figured out," nor do I proclaim to be an expert in all things business-related. I'm not going to pretend that I know it all, because I don't; and I don't want the pressure of thinking I should... I learned to let go of that expectation years ago.

Rather, I'm on this journey *with* you, and it's my intent to share what has worked for me, my six—and seven—figure clients, and my colleagues.

CHAPTER 2
THE AUTOMATE YOUR GROWTH
FORMULA

This book is based on the Automate Your Growth™ Formula, which is made up of the three key elements required to run a business that serves you.

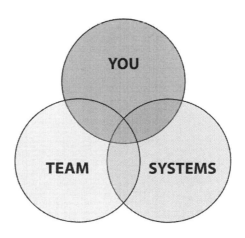

1) **You**–What do you want to create? And what is your role in doing so? How might you get in your own way when it comes to creating the success you want? (We are our own worst enemies at times; I know that from personal experience!)

2) **Systems**–I believe strong business systems are the key to success and sanity in business. With a strong foundation of systems in place, you are able to grow a business that will serve both you and your clients in the best way possible.

3) **Team**–Regardless of the type of business you want, it's impossible to do it all alone. But how do you know who you need to hire – and better yet, who not to hire? Where do you find great people, and how can you lead a great team?

I first created this formula when I ran a workshop in 2011 called How to Set Up Your Business to Run without You. Because that is what this is really all about. Too many entrepreneurs suffer from the following scenario:

- You start out in your business on your own, without much money to spend on systems or team, so you tend to do a lot of the work yourself.
- Your business starts to grow, and even though you are getting busy, you are still able to keep up with everything that needs to get done.
- Then you start to get really busy and would like some help, but you aren't sure what else you need (Who do you need to hire? What systems do you need to put in place?), so you keep on juggling to hold it all together.
- Things are hopping – you have some team members in place and have started to put some systems in place, too, but you are still the one in the center involved in almost everything that is going on in the business.

In other words, **if you weren't there, the entire thing would fall apart—everything is coming to you and through you.**

Consider the diagram below. You are the biggest piece of the pie and your "arms" are around the team and systems holding it all together. Tiring!!

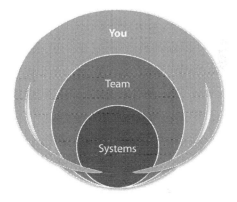

What we are aiming for is the opposite. Instead of the above, imagine that your business could look like this instead:

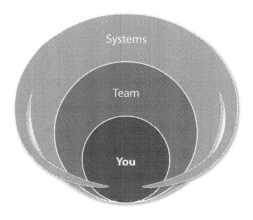

The systems are the biggest piece of the pie. With the right systems in place—centralizing, automating, and documenting (which we'll talk about later)—you are able to do less in the business. In fact, with the support of great systems and a team that runs those systems, you get to be the smallest piece of the pie. You get to do the things that you do best—the stuff you really enjoy and that grows your business— instead of trying to do it all.

Did I just hear a sigh of relief?

The Way You Run Your Business Will Make or Break You

You can run your business in one of two ways:

1) **Reactive mode** is when you just "go with the flow,"— when you don't really have a plan, you just react to what comes your way and deal with it when it does.
2) **Proactive mode** is when you take the time to consider what you want, lay out a plan, and prepare as much as possible for each step that is coming your way.

All of us start our businesses in reactive mode—it's just a natural part of starting a business. Start-up mode is what I call *stage 1* of business growth, and is all about experimentation and proving your business model. You have an idea of what you want to offer and who you want to work with, but quite often things evolve as you try different ideas and have varying levels of success. This stage requires you to be a bit reactive—to be able to respond to feedback you receive so you can figure out the business model and shift into growth mode.

Once you have proven your business model—people are buying what you are offering—then you are in *stage 2* of business growth, in which the focus is to continue to build on that foundation.

14

Ideally, as you shift from stage 1 to stage 2, you also shift from being reactive to being proactive. Instead of flying by the seat of your pants, you start to plan ahead. You take the time to decide what you want to do in the coming months and years, and work together with your team to make it happen.

How do you know whether or not you are in reactive mode? As my Online Business Manager, Tiffany, says:

"If you go to bed tonight not knowing what you are doing in the morning, then you are in reactive mode."

Couldn't say it better myself. ☺

A big goal of this book is to help you shift from reactive mode to proactive mode, and to give you the tools to do so. Not shifting from reactive mode to proactive mode is what causes A LOT of issues for entrepreneurs at this stage of growth. And many people aren't sure exactly why they are struggling, let alone how to fix it.

A few things to consider when it comes to shifting from reactive to proactive mode:

- **Being reactive is much easier**—it's a lot easier to simply go with the flow and respond to what comes to you versus stepping back and considering what you really want and how to get there. Reactive mode is a hard habit to break for many of us, especially if we have been stuck there for years.

- **Reactive mode can feel "good enough"**—this is a very dangerous trap in my opinion, and one that I found myself in for many years. I was the queen of flying by the seat of my pants and taking whatever opportunity came my way. And quite honestly, it was

OK. I was making decent money and enjoying my work for the most part. But it really wasn't by design, and it got to the point where I felt like something was missing. I no longer wanted to just grab what came to me. I started to get the itch to create work that I really wanted to do. And it was then that my whole business model and income changed (more on that in the next chapter).

- **Reactive mode can actually be a lot of fun**—there is a rush from the energy of "go go go!!!" that comes into play when you are in reactive mode. Although it can be draining and frustrating, it can also be exciting to get up each day not knowing what will come your way and just having to go with it. It can be very fulfilling to tackle the unexpected and come out on top.

- **Reactive mode affects everyone in your business**—it's not just about you. If you are in reactive mode it forces your team to always be in reactive mode as well, continually scrambling to catch up, put out fires, and try to get things done right and on time.

I believe that many entrepreneurs are addicted to chaos, which is a huge side effect of being in reactive mode. I'm certainly no psychologist or scientist, and thus can't speak to this from that perspective... I just know what I've experienced myself and seen with many of my clients over the years.

I have an addictive personality in many ways, and I know I was addicted to the chaos for many years in my business. I'm very good at creating order out of chaos—it's actually a strength of mine—and so I would feed off that and purposely put myself in those situations. Even though I might complain about it, I also really loved the excitement and uncertainty of it all. I loved getting up in the morning and being surprised by what I found in my inbox. I loved having a problem thrown at me and having to scramble to figure it out. It really was a kind of high for me.

So this is something to be aware of when it comes to your own business. Do you get high from the chaos? What would it feel like to run your business differently? Does the thought of not being in reactive mode feel like relief or disappointment? The first step is awareness—to see if you are someone who thrives on chaos. If yes, then the steps I outline in this book will probably feel uncomfortable to you at times as you start to apply them. But I can say from experience that getting to the other side is a much more pleasant and sane way to run your business.

Planning 3 Steps Ahead

One of the key elements of being able to shift into proactive mode is to plan ahead.

I'm not a fan of the traditional business plan in which you plan out your business a year or two or three in advance. And yes, I know many people out there disagree with me, some vehemently so. But I find it hard to plan too far in advance, for the simple fact that I don't always know what my clients (and what I!) will want a year from now. Maybe it's just my rebellious nature, but the idea of mapping out the next three years makes me want to run screaming. But I know it's important to plan ahead or I will always be in reactive mode.

Instead, I like to use what I call the *3 Steps Ahead Strategy*, which means that I always know what the next three things are that are coming down the pipeline, regardless of the timing of them.

17

I run a training and speaking business, which means that we launch various training programs throughout the year. When I apply the 3 Steps Ahead Strategy, it means that we are currently launching Training A, then after that I know that we will be launching Training B, then C, and D. I know what the next three things are that we will be doing, which might span the next three months or the next six months. It means we can map out a plan for success and get the pieces in place now versus always having everything come up at the last minute and always trying to catch up.

So what is your 3 Steps Ahead Strategy? If you aren't clear on your next three steps, I invite you to consider them and make appropriate decisions. And of course you are welcome to plan more than three steps ahead if that suits your business. But make sure it is at least three steps. Once you have done so, post the steps on your wall to keep them front of mind, and share them with your team. This will become the foundation for creating success via your systems and team as we'll discuss in future chapters.

Your Commitment

There are a few commitments that I ask of you as you work through this book and put the Automate Your Growth Formula to work for you and your business:

- Commit to putting yourself first, so you create a business you really want versus one that you think you should want or that others want for you.
- Commit to consciously making the shift from reactive to proactive mode, even if it makes you cringe right now.
- Commit to taking your business seriously and putting the right systems and team in place. I don't care if it's just you offering a one-to-one service to your clients,

or building an empire... you honor your business, your clients, and yourself when you take these steps.

- Commit to saying no if something truly doesn't fit for you. I think *no* is one of the most underutilized words in the entrepreneur's vocabulary and that many entrepreneurs get themselves into all kinds of traps but not using it often enough. This applies to this book or any other kind of business advice you receive—you have every right to say no to what doesn't fit for you.

CHAPTER 3
WHAT KIND OF BUSINESS
DO YOU *REALLY* WANT?

I am amazed by how many people I know who are trapped in businesses that they actually never wanted in the first place, simply because they weren't clear on what they really wanted or got caught up in looking at others around them and feeling like they should do the same thing.

Take, for example, my friend Bryn Johnson of BrynJohnson.com:

> "After leaving my corporate job at Monster.com in 2010 I was ready to devote myself to my business and invested heavily in coaching and support to do so. After a couple of years I found myself miserable—I was making money hand over fist with amazing clients but was not motivated by

my work at all. I came to realize that I had hired a staff to build a business with me that I didn't want.

After coming dangerously close to burnout I took some time to get quiet and pay attention to what I really loved doing. I had actually known all along what I really wanted to do but had given that up for the "sexy business model" that so many others were touting. I realized that in paying attention to those around me I had ignored my own inner voice. I've since shifted my business model to do the things I love to do the most (and which had been a big part of my success in the corporate world)—speaking and writing. Once I made the decision to do what I really wanted the opportunities came pouring in—such as being invited to be an expert blogger for Monster and to host my own radio show. I'm now loving my business for the first time ever."

In this chapter I want you to explore what kind of business you really want and why, and this starts with exploring your *why*.

Step #1: Why Did You Start Your Business?

There are three common *whys* for entrepreneurs when it comes to starting a business:

- Freedom–being able to do what you want when you want to do it
- Money–making as much as possible in order to enjoy everything it allows you to have in life
- Meaning–being able to serve from your purpose, helping people in the way that you were meant to do so

Each of us has a driving why, and probably a bit of the other two as well.

Freedom is my driving why. I created my business for the simple fact that I hate it when people tell me what to do (my first word as a child was "no"—go figure!). I don't want someone to tell me I have to do X or be somewhere at a certain time... and I certainly don't want someone to tell me what I have to wear! (You want me to wear pantyhose? No thanks!) I like to be able to do what I want to do with my time, be it working or not (hence the reason I take a firm stand on not working weekends). I like to be able to express myself the way I want to through my work instead of trying to fit into someone else's mold. This is why I consider myself unemployable these days (LOL).

Meaning is my secondary why, as I simply can't sustain doing work that has no meaning. I remember this from my days of being employed, in particular with my first job as an accounts payable clerk for the head office of a large grocery chain. Yes, the work was necessary to the running of the business. But what kind of impact was I having on the world at large? What difference did it really make if I was good at my job or not? I simply wasn't motivated to be the best darn accounts payable clerk in the world. Fast-forward to my work today as an entrepreneur... I LOVE the fact that the work I do has an impact. I love when someone says something to me like, "Tina, because of your program I'm able to take a vacation with my family for the first time in three years." Or "After reading your book I finally know what I want to do. Thank you!" The work that I do matters, and that is really important to me.

Money is the why that's third on my list. And I've come to realize that it's not actually that important to me. Don't get me wrong; I love money and enjoy all that it allows for me, my family, and my business. But it simply isn't my driving force, and anytime I've tried to do something simply for the money, it wasn't enough to motivate me. I've tried to set goals based on money alone, but if they aren't led by freedom and meaning, then they simply fizzle out.

What is most important to you? What is your why?

It might have been a while since you considered this for yourself. Or this might be the first time ever. If you feel unsure about your why, try stepping back a bit and looking at decisions you've made in the past. It was actually only recently that I realized that freedom is my driving why—up until that point I would have said meaning was the first one. But when I realized how many times I've made decisions in life based on freedom, it was obvious. And since then I've come to use it as a touchstone for all that I do. The reason I had to write this book is to help you get more freedom along with money and meaning.

When you are clear on your why, it will help to define everything else in your business, including how much time, money, and effort you are willing to put in (or sacrifice) to create the level of success you want.

For example, someone who is driven by freedom may not be willing to work lots of hours, whereas someone driven more by money might be totally fine with working many hours in order to reach their financial goals. Someone driven by meaning might be OK with sacrificing certain things in life in order to fulfill what really matters to them.

Your why becomes the touchstone for making decisions about how to run your business.

Step #2: Decide What Business Model You Want

Do you want to be self-employed? Or do you want a legacy-style business?

- Self-employed means that you are the one *doing* the work in the business—usually a service-based business such as massage therapist, graphic designer, copywriter, virtual assistant, or dog groomer. *Doing* can also apply to a retail or product-based business if you are still the one doing all the work (that is, if you are the one in the store all day). When you are self-employed, you generally function as a solopreneur, meaning that you do most (if not all) of the work for your clients and that you may have a bit of help behind the scenes, but not much.
- A legacy-style business means that your business becomes bigger than you. You can no longer do it all on your own, and need the right systems and team around you to continue to grow. This can apply to product- or service-based businesses that are ready to grow to the next level.

One is not better than the other—I just want to be clear about that. This is strictly about you making a conscious decision based on what you want. (After all, this is YOUR business and YOUR life.)

Some key considerations:

- Time—how much time do you want to dedicate to your business based on your commitments and lifestyle? There is a big difference between someone who is single and has no family commitments to consider and a mom with a family to consider.

- Effort–how much energy do you have to devote to your business right now? If you have other major stressors in your life, you will want to balance that with the type of business you are creating.

- Money–how much money do you want to make? How much money are you willing to invest in your business? Being self-employed generally means earning less money than a legacy-style business, but it requires less money (fewer expenses) to run the business.

Let's compare what this mean in the two types of business models:

	Self-Employed	**Legacy**
Pros	• Easy to start • Easier to run (usually just you!) • All the money you make is yours (minimal expenses)	• No cap on time or availability (replicate delivery via products or associates) • Unlimited opportunity for income • A saleable business • You are able to focus on key areas
Cons	• Your income is limited by your availability to do the work • Can be hard to balance all elements of biz • A tendency to think you have to do it all • Not usually a saleable business.	• Requires strong systems and team • Requires willingness to invest in biz (money and time) • Can easily overwhelm you if you stay stuck in the middle

Most entrepreneurs start with being self-employed and then may grow into a legacy-style business down the road.

I was self-employed for many years in my business—strictly self-employed from 1999 to 2005 when I worked as a freelancer and Online Business Manager (OBM). I was a bit of both from 2005 to 2009, when I started doing training programs and writing books while still working as an OBM for a few clients. Then, as of 2009, I officially stopped working as an OBM and shifted my business 100 percent into legacy mode.

I was VERY happy being self-employed for those early years—I loved the fact that I got to do great work with great clients. Although I had commitments and responsibilities, I also had the freedom of working from home, working when I wanted to work (or not working when I didn't want to!), and being able to make a good living. My girls were born in 2006 and 2008, and I was able to continue to work part-time and enjoy those precious early years with them.

Then in 2009 I got what I like to call *the itch*—my girls were one and three—still young, but past the newborn have-to-be-with-Mommy-24/7 stage. I had launched my first book, *Becoming an Online Business Manager*, in the fall of 2008, and was getting a great response to the book and the accompanying OBM Certification Training program I had developed. I loved my OBM clients, but was honestly starting to get bored being an OBM for them. I just had a feeling in my gut that it was time for the next stage of growth in my business. In the summer of 2009, I made the decision to officially let go of the last of my OBM clients and focus solely on building my legacy-style training business.

BEWARE: It is really easy to fall into what I call the *You aren't successful until you hit six or seven figures* trap.

I get so annoyed with all of the "Here's what you need to do to hit six figures!" or "You haven't made it until you hit seven figures" stuff out there. It's easy to look around, see what someone else is doing, and think, "I should do that, too." Or to have someone tell you, "This is the type of business you need to create."

I talk to people all the time who are doing very well with their self-employed business model and say, "I want to hit six figures." And the first words out of my mouth are, "Beware of what you wish for." **The more money you make, the more responsibility you have in a business,** and this is something that I wasn't really prepared for when I decided to shift from self-employed to legacy.

When I was self-employed, I only had to be responsible for myself, my commitments, and delivering great work to my clients. Outside of a few small business expenses, all the money I made essentially went to my pocket. And if I didn't make a lot of money, it was fine, as I didn't need a lot of money.

When I shifted to legacy mode, I was literally unable to do all the work myself anymore, nor did I want to. So I had to hire more help. I had already been working with a great virtual assistant part time, but I decided it was time to hire my own Online Business Manager. I hired Tiffany in January of 2010, and she's still with me today!

I also joined a mastermind program and hired a coach to help me work to the next level in my business. I started travelling more, upgraded my website and materials, invested in newer systems, hired lawyers to create agreements, and so on. Needless to say, all of these things cost money, and I found myself with real business expenses for the first time.

Now I felt the pressure to make money to cover these expenses. No longer could I just mosey along... I had to take my business seriously! And although I never got into any real trouble, I certainly found it uncomfortable at times. There were days when I yearned for my old self-employed life, when I just did work for my clients, got paid, and that was it.

This is why I always recommend that someone gives it serious thought before they decide to make the shift to legacy. **Don't do it just because you think you should or someone told you that you should build your business a certain way**. Do it because you want to – because you feel an internal calling or purpose to do so. Otherwise you might find yourself in a business that you don't want.

You also want to consider your exit plan. Your time in your business will come to an end at some point in your journey, which is something you may not have thought about before (or may not want to think about).Consider your long-term plans. How would you like to end this business? For most people it is either:

a) Selling the business—there is a payout, and you may or may not still be involved in the business.

b) Retiring the business—when you are done, the business shuts down (common in service-based businesses), in which case you want to be saving and planning for your retirement during the life of your business.

c) Transferring the business—you might want to pass the business along to your family or children, in which case you will need to start planning for this now and grooming them for takeover.

There are various considerations that come into play here, the most obvious of which is money. It's easy for entrepreneurs to chug along putting off saving money or considering their retirement.

Paying Yourself First

I remember the first year I first made six figures in my business. A part of me was excited and proud! I had never thought that I would be someone who hit the six-figure mark, so it was pretty darn cool to have done so. But on the other hand it was a bit of a letdown, as I didn't actually have more money in my personal bank account. In order to hit six figures I had to spend more money in the business, and ended up with less for me.

My coach at the time suggested that I start paying myself first and create a wealth account. So I decided to take 10 percent of my revenues each month and pay myself first. Now I will tell you this was pretty hard some months. I would look at my other business expenses and commitments and think, "I can't do it! If I pay myself first, I might not have money for A, B, or C." But I did it anyway, and a couple of things happened:

- Somehow I always had the money to pay for all my other expenses. Even though I was afraid at times to do so, when I stuck to my commitment to payment myself first I was always able to make enough money to pay for the rest.
- At the end of the year I had multiple five figures sitting in my wealth account, and it felt damn good! If I had continued on as I had the year before, I wouldn't have had anything in there, and it was that money that allowed my husband and I to decide to take the risk of having him quit his job and join the business in the fall of 2011—we had enough financial cushion for him to do so.

Money is like time. There is no end to what you can spend it on. And if you don't get into the habit of paying yourself first, you may find yourself years down the road with a successful business BUT no money for yourself and no exit plan that will pay you for all of your years of hard work. And that would be a bummer.

Step #3: Decide What You Will (and Won't) Offer to Your Clients.

Now that you've decided what business model you want, it's time to take a look at what you are offering.

For many of my clients, the first step is to take a look at their business to date and make some decisions—to consider what they have been offering and how they have been working with clients.

- What has worked (or not worked)?
- What clients do I enjoy working with (or not)?
- Do I like how I have been packaging my services and offerings?
- Is there anything I want to change (do more or less of)?
- Is there anything new I want to offer?
- Is there anything I simply no longer enjoy doing and want to stop doing?

Before you continue to grow, you want to make sure that you grow on the *right* foundation – and by right I mean the right one for you and your business.

For many of us the issue isn't lack of options, but having way too many! There are literally hundreds of ways you can make money in a business these days, and you need to decide what you will and won't offer. And in my experience there are usually several options that will achieve the same goal.

I can't tell you how many times over the years I've had people tell me, "Tina, you should hire your own team of OBMs that people can hire from you." But you know what? I don't want that kind of business. I get that the opportunity exists, and that I'm well positioned to create that kind of business and be pretty darn successful at it, but it doesn't light my fire.

This was the reason why many years ago I decided to start an OBM Certification and Training Program rather than create my own team-based business. I enjoy training, speaking, writing, and mentoring, and have built my business offerings on those things. This has fulfilled my mission on that side of the business, which is to give support professionals the opportunity to work at a higher level with their clients by becoming OBMs, and to give business owners the higher level of support they need in their businesses by hiring an OBM.

Either way would have achieved that same goal, but one would have made me miserable.

Another example is a decision that my friend Milana Leshinsky of Milana.com made in her business:

> "I've tried doing live events, masterminds and big ticket programs like many other coaches out there. But you know what? I didn't enjoy them at all. I didn't enjoy delivering in-depth coaching programs with a client for ten months. I didn't enjoy the stress of producing my own live event. Instead I enjoy creating trainings and programs that people can use when they need them.
>
> I've come to embrace the fact that I like to work in bursts. The launch model is perfect for me as I get to spend two months preparing, launching, run the

program and done! Then I will take a break for a few months and take it easy before my next launch. This model allows me to keep a focus on my family and make enough money to enjoy our lifestyle."

Another common trap is the keep-doing-it-because-people-are-buying-it trap. On one hand this is smart business, and I certainly wouldn't recommend cutting off your nose to spite your face! But I know many people who continue to do stuff in their businesses that they no longer enjoy, and continue to work with clients they actually can't stand, because it makes them money or they think they should. (Sounds an awful lot like having a job, doesn't it?)

I've found that there are seasons in our businesses, and we need to step back and take inventory when we are coming to the end of a season to ensure that we continue to build something we enjoy and want. It is when we are shifting from one season to the next that we get to make choices – which can be both exciting and scary!

I run on a three-year cycle. I'm very much a starter and a finisher, but I'm not a maintainer. So I like to create things and bring them to life and to completion... I like to do the work for a while, but once it's set up and running, well, I'm ready for the next thing.

For example, in 2011 I found myself getting bored with my OBM Certification and Training Program – the thing I had poured my heart and soul into for three years! At first I resisted the boredom. How could I be tired of what I considered (at the time) to be my life's work? I love my OBMs and want to support them. I believe wholeheartedly in providing this training. But I was tired of delivering the same program over and over again. It was actually my OBM Tiffany who found the heart of the issue when she said:"Tina, you need a new problem to solve."

It was like a lightning bolt hit me—she was bang on.

I'm a problem solver. I LOVE to solve problems. Math was my favorite subject in school. And once I've solved a problem like creating a training program that allows people to become OBMs, I'm ready to move onto the next problem.

And—more important—that doesn't mean that I have to put an end to what I've already created. I was not going to stop offering the OBM program, as I knew how valuable it was and I was totally committed to everyone on that journey. I just had to change my part in it so that the training could go on without me and I could focus some of my energy elsewhere. I realized I could still work with OBMs, but in a different way via our mentorship and other training programs. We decided to automate the OBM training and have Tiffany take over as training manager, which took some time to set up but has been working out very well.

If you find yourself no longer enjoying the things that make you money, you have a couple of options:

- Look at how you can restructure so that you can continue to offer those elements of your business, but without your involvement. This might be automating a program or perhaps hiring someone to do the work that you are doing now (like Tiffany and I did).

- You might want to stop offering a service altogether. Sometimes it makes sense to let something go in order to focus on something new or different, and of course you have every right to do so! I always recommend that you plan out about six months to a year for transferring from the old to the new so that you don't find yourself in a cash crunch or crisis.

Step #4: Creating Your YES! List

Now that you are clear on your business model and what you want to offer, it's time to get clear on what you should and should not be doing in your business. What should be on your plate?

The first step in automating and hiring a team (which of course we'll talk about in depth in later chapters) is to know what your own role is in the business.

There are two types of things that should be on your plate:

1. **The stuff you love doing** –This may be obvious, but I want to make sure that you are able to do the things you love in your business. After all, this is probably why you chose the type of business you chose, right? So I want you to create as much space as possible to do the things you love.
2. **The stuff that grows your business (even if you don't love it)**–You need to own the marketing and sales activities that will continue to grow your business, even if you would rather not do them. You cannot delegate the success of your business; no one else will care about it as much as you do.

Even if it sucks, and part of you cringes, you need to own the marketing and sales process in your business. If you aren't very good at it yet, you need to get good – there are a myriad of resources, training, and people out there to help you with this. Then, once you've nailed down what works and doesn't work in growing your business (that is, you've proven your strategies make money), then you can look at getting some help with it. But you always want to have your finger on the pulse of marketing and sales.

35

A caveat here: Beware of the things you love to do but are not actually growing your business! You may need to get some of these things off your plate in order to create space for the stuff that really matters. I remember a client years ago who shared that she had recently hired a bookkeeper – not because she hated doing the books, but because she loved it! She would distract herself with bookkeeping when she should have been focused on marketing or making a sales call.

What might be a distraction for you? Make a list so you can catch yourself doing it. I'm a techie geek at heart, and I love to mess around in systems and such, so I have to be very purposeful in not letting myself get distracted by playing around in Infusionsoft or tweaking my website. I will admit to having my geek-out moments, but for the most part I'm pretty good at letting my team take care of those things for me now (and I know to expect a loving slap on the wrist when I stick my nose in where it shouldn't be!☺

How to Create Your YES! List

This is something I have all my clients do—so simple and very effective. First, write out a list of the things that should be on your plate based on the above. For many entrepreneurs the list will look something like this:

- Big Picture Vision and Strategy–making the big decisions in your business

- Marketing and Sales (for now)–need a strong, proven marketing process before outsourcing

- Content Creation–writing articles, blog posts, videos, and new products and offerings

- Delivery of Services–coaching, teaching, designing, etc.

- Joint Venture Relationships–finding and building relationships with key partners to support your growth

- Speaking and Teaching–exposure and credibility

Write your list on a big sheet of paper or a whiteboard and post it right beside your desk. It needs to be somewhere obvious where you can see it at a glance. Then, throughout the day, ask yourself, "Is this on my YES! List?" If it is, keep on doing it. If not, it is something you need to get off your plate, and I'll show you how to do so in future chapters.

Bottom line here is this: *You* get to decide what kind of business you want to create and how it fits into your life. Although I always recommend listening to the advice of people who have credibility in what they offer (they've proven their own success), don't let other people tell you what you should do in your business.

Do a gut check and ask yourself, "Is this the type of business I want to build? Does this excite me?" If the answer is no, you need to go back to the drawing board. There is simply no way to sustain the energy it takes to build a business that you don't really want. Nor should you have to!

CHAPTER 4
TAKING BACK YOUR TIME
(NO MORE WORKING WEEKENDS!)

How much time will you work (or not) in a week? Are you working too much? Do you work on the weekends?

Working on weekends is an epidemic right now for many entrepreneurs, and one that needs to stop. People are working *way* too many hours in their businesses – evenings, weekends, or until the wee hours of the morning – and that is simply nutty.

How do I know? I talk to people all the time who are working too much and are exhausted, frustrated, and stressed, but don't know how to stop. I'm here to help with that. ☺

First, a quick assessment to see if you are working too much:

Is Work Taking Over your Life? Check all that apply:

- You wake up in the morning and the first thing you do is check your email.
- You keep your cell phone by your bedside and wake up to check it throughout the night.
- You are out for dinner and keep your cell phone beside your plate in case something comes in.
- Your cell phone rings or you get a text and you answer it even if you are in the middle of something else.
- You feel lost if you aren't able to check your email.
- Your stomach is rumbling because you didn't have breakfast before starting to work, and it's now noon.
- It's 2:00 p.m. and you still haven't taken that shower that you meant to take at 8:00 a.m.
- It's not unusual for you to be working late at night or until the wee hours of the morning.
- You work weekends on a regular basis.
- You never take breaks throughout the day and will work until you drop.
- When a client or colleague asks you for something you immediately say yes without considering your schedule.
- Your spouse or kids ask when you will get off the computer to spend time with them.
- You find yourself saying, "I just have to do one more thing and I'll be right there"... and thirty minutes later you are still working.
- You haven't taken a real, unplugged vacation in a long time (could be years!).
- You go on vacation but take your laptop and/or cell phone with you to do some work.
- Regardless of how much you work, it feels like you can never catch up.

☐ You are exhausted from working so much.

☐ You can't stop thinking about work, even when you aren't working.

☐ You get emotional (even break out in tears) because you are so stressed out about your workload.

☐ You miss your old life and some days wish you hadn't started your business.

Add up your score _____

0 to 5–Manageable. I would still suggest working on these areas, but you are probably in a pretty good place.

5 to 10–Fixable. You can probably get away with it for now, but things will start to catch up with you.

10+–Crisis Mode. You need to look at making some changes soon before your business sucks the life out of you! (And just so you know you aren't alone... many people score over 10.)

What Sparked This Movement for Me

A few years ago, I got to work Monday morning and saw an email from a business colleague that said, "Hey, I'm doing a training series and I'm looking for presenters... if you are interested let me know. I'm looking for forty(ish) speakers and I'm going to fill spaces first come first served." The email was dated Saturday morning, and here it was Monday morning. So I thought, "Great! I'll be one of the first to reply," and popped off an email. A short while later I got an email from her saying "Sorry, all the spots were filled on the weekend." I remember pausing and thinking, "WTF? Am I the only person not working on the weekends?" That was the first time this really hit home for me. I had no idea that so many people were working on the weekends! Since then I've talked to many of my clients, colleagues, and fellow entrepreneurs who are working weekends even when they don't want to.

This annoys the heck out of me. I believe we *deserve* to have time in our lives when we are not working, and I believe that weekends are the best (and most natural) option. I don't know about you, but I didn't work weekends when I had a regular day job, so why the heck would I set myself up to always have to work weekends in my business?

Yes, I love my work. Yes, I love my clients. But as I've already shared, **I love my freedom more... and that's the reason I started my business.**

I'm talking about taking weekends off, but for you it might be different. You might decide that you prefer to take time off throughout the week instead, or maybe take off an entire week each month. So long as you are purposeful in taking dedicated, meaningful time off from your business, then you are on the right track.

For example, Kendall SummerHawk[1] shared with me how she makes her horses a priority in her schedule. Spending time with her horses is a passion, not a hobby, and they come first each day. Because of where she lives, she needs to work with her horses in the morning because it's too hot in the afternoon, so she keeps her mornings free from work and doesn't arrive at her office until 11:00 a.m. Her team knows this and will not schedule anything for her before that time. And you know what? With this schedule she has been able to create a highly successful multi-seven-figure business and serve her mission of being the premier coaching training

---

[1] Of KendallSummerhawk.com

organization for women. Not working in the morning hasn't gotten in the way of her success at all.

Don't get me wrong... I've done the working weekends thing. And for a while it was fine—until it wasn't anymore. I did it for many years, actually. And it got to the point where I felt like I was always working—that I didn't have anything in my life other than work (because I didn't, really).

So I ask you: Do you want to work on the weekends?

Time is one of the most precious commodities we have, and we all get the exact same amount. How you spend your time is up to you.

Many of the people I talk to are working on the weekends because they feel like they *have* to rather than *want* to. They feel as though they need to use that time to catch up or they would never be able to get done what needs to be done. They feel as though they would be missing out on something if they weren't continually plugged into their business. They feel the pressure from clients, customers, team members, or colleagues to "do it all," and feel like they have no other choice but to work on the weekends.

But in reality they would *love* to not work on the weekends—to take that time back and enjoy life outside of work—to enjoy time with family (especially for those of us with kids!), for hobbies, or even just to relax and do nothing (one of my favorite things to do).

They find themselves stuck in what I call the *working weekends trap*, and aren't sure how to stop. (I'll tell you how below.)

Maybe you are good with working on weekends, and that's totally fine as long as it's a conscious choice and not just something you are tolerating. Before you officially make that decision, I want to review some of the most common reasons I hear from entrepreneurs about working on the weekends.

"I love my work and enjoy it!"

Even if you love your work (as I do), that doesn't mean you should be doing it 24/7. I love chocolate, but if I have it too often it can make me sick. Even healthy things can cause issues if we go overboard with them. For example, someone who enjoys running but does too much of it can end up injured. The same thing applies to your work – if you work too much too often, it can be damaging:

- **You may be hurting relationships with your family and friends,** who don't get enough time and attention from you. Every time you check your phone or do "just one small thing" when you are supposed to be focused on your family means you are choosing work over them.

- **There are serious health risks that come into play with overworking yourself and being in a constant state of stress**. Physical burnout is a very real thing, and can have serious consequences manifesting in things like insomnia, chronic fatigue, weight gain, and anxiety issues. Some believe it even contributes to things like type 2 diabetes and other long-term health issues.

(NOTE: I am in no way a health professional. I'm just sharing some of what I've read and what other people in the health industry have shared with me. If you have ANY concerns about physical burnout, please be sure to contact your doctor or a medical professional right away.)

- **You will no longer be as effective**. If you are always on the go, you simply won't be able to do as good a job as you would if you had regular and adequate breaks in your work schedule. Rest is necessary to do good work.

- **You may even find yourself starting to resent the work that you once used to love simply because you've had too much of it** (like eating too much turkey at Thanksgiving dinner: It was so good, you couldn't stop, and now you can't stand the thought of another bite).

I also believe that magic happens when we purposely give ourselves a break and unplug from our businesses on a regular basis. Even though I don't work weekends and rarely even think about work on the weekends anymore, I feel that some of my best ideas and solutions come from the time I'm unplugged. It's almost as though my subconscious has the space to breathe and allow things to come together in a way that they simply would not if I were continually go-go-go!

"I have to work on the weekends or I will never get it all done."

Believe me, guys, I get it—you are busy, and it can certainly feel impossible to get everything done the way things are now, let alone deciding to no longer work weekends!

For some of you, simple math comes into play – you literally have too many things on your plate and need to review what you should and shouldn't be doing (creating your YES! List).**When you get clear on the best use of your time in your business, you can then work towards putting the right systems and team in place to take care**

45

of the rest. This is essential for any growing business and we'll certainly cover this in a later chapter.

Assuming that your current workload is realistic, I want to introduce you to Parkinson's Law, which states:

Work expands so as to fill the time available for its completion.[2]

Essentially what this means is that whatever time you allow yourself for work, you will find work to fill that time. If you set up your schedule to include weekends, evenings, and into the wee hours of the morning, you will ALWAYS find work to do in that time.

You finish one thing and the next thing pops up on the list. If you are setting your work schedule based on the amount of work you have on your plate, that is essentially a recipe for insanity—because you will never reach the end of your list!

The other side of Parkinson's Law is what truly gives you freedom and allows you to take back your time. When you allocate certain days and times to get the work done, you will find that you are able to get it done in that time frame.

In other words, give yourself a deadline or a time frame in which to do the work and you will make it happen. We've all had deadlines that were tight or seemed almost impossible to meet, but somehow we did it. This is because "the work expanded (or in this case contracted) to fit the time that we allowed for it."

---

[2]http://en.wikipedia.org/wiki/Parkinson's_law

Applying Parkinson's Law also forces us to stop doing the little things and busy work that can take up a surprising amount of time in our day. Are you aware of how much time you spend checking email, playing on social media sites, or just generally fussing around during your workday? For many entrepreneurs this adds up to hours a week, and in some cases many hours a day.

This might sound crazy to you, and I get it... it doesn't make "logical" sense. But I've seen it work time and time again for my clients and I've experienced it myself.

Let me share with you Tiffany's story...

"I started my business in 2008 as a VA/OBM and very quickly had a full practice. However, it didn't take long for me to realize that there was a learning curve, and though clients were easy to get, I needed to be able to fully support them. Saying no was an issue for me (as I wanted to help everyone). **Ultimately I had way more clients, with way more commitments, than there was time in a day.** But you couldn't tell me that because I was determined... I had "caught scent" of the success I wanted and nothing was going to deter me from my vision.

So I dug in and worked hard, from 8:00 a.m. to 2:00 a.m., for months at a time. (Keep in mind I am a wife and mother of two, and I am not proud of the fact that those I love the most suffered for my determination.) I would work weekends, holidays, and vacations. Honestly, I went from cooking dinner four or five nights of the week to cooking dinner once every four or five months. I basically shut out all of my "real life" friends (you know, the coffee dates with the gals or couples' card night with friends). I was determined to build what I could envision as my business success. Three years passed and thirty-five pounds were added. (Yep... sitting in front of the computer for fourteen hours a day is not good for the waistline.)

By this time my business had evolved to doing what I do love the most – working as an Online Business Manager. **But I had hit a point at which I was so burned out, physically and creatively drained, that I was ready to throw in the towel.** Although I was exhausted, I did not see another option. I simply could not continue. If you have ever been there, you know this is a sickening pain in the most intimate part of you. I had worked so hard to build something I could love, working with great clients so I would feel successful, yet there was nothing left in me to enjoy it.

Then I went on a mentorship retreat surrounded by my OBM peers and my mentor, friend (and client), Tina Forsyth. **It was at this retreat that I hit my breaking point. I literally broke down in tears because I knew I could not continue the way I was going.** I fully saw how broken I was and the break I needed from my business. In the course of this mastermind event, we mapped out a plan that had me working 8:00 a.m. to 4:00 p.m., Monday thru Friday *only*... a plan that had me doing what I really loved to do—a plan that was (though I didn't know it at the time) going to save my business and keep me from being a failure. It was a good plan and I made a commitment to it.

Now, more than a year later, I *love, love, love* my business. I *never* work weekends, and I am out of my office by 5:00 p.m. most days. I go to *all* of my kids' events, and I even cook dinner several times a week. I have rekindled friendships that had faded, and always make the *relationships* in my life a priority. Don't get me wrong, I still work hard... just not on the weekends. I think before I say yes (asking myself, 'Does this really support my overall goal?'). I do not break my boundaries anymore as I see them as promises to my family. I rely on the amazing support I have on my team (this was probably the hardest for a control freak like me to do), and I make time for the fun I want in my life."

As I've mentioned already, Tiffany is my Online Business Manager and has worked with me since January of 2010. Here's a key point that I want to make:

When Tiffany started working Monday to Friday and taking weekends off she became *much* more effective in her work. I could see it from the other side; things that had been slipping or balls that were being dropped were all improved. Projects that had sat on the sidelines for months were being completed. When she stopped working too many hours she was able to get more work done (and I was a happier client for it). ☺

Bottom line is this: You get to choose. Regardless of how much work is on your plate and how much it might feel like you "just have to do it now," it is ultimately a choice. If you don't want to work on weekends you don't have to, so here are five tips for taking your time back:

#1: Get clear on your NON-working hours.

A lot of people talk about setting your working hours, and although I believe this is important, I think it's more important to decide your NON-working hours. I know for many entrepreneurs, myself included, it's not about working a normal 9:00 a.m. to 5:00 p.m. day. There are times when we have to work evenings or maybe get up a bit earlier to finish something.

In the spirit of not working too much, the most important question you can ask yourself is: **When will I NOT work?**

You might decide that you won't work on weekends. Maybe it's evenings, and you will shut off your computer at 6:30 p.m. for the night. Or you might say that you won't work between 4:00 p.m. and 8:00 p.m. each day to spend time with your family, but that it's OK to hop back on the computer after that if need be.

Again, you get to choose—there really aren't any right or wrong choices as long as you have *some* non-working time built in on your calendar.

My non-working hours are weekends and before 9:00 a.m. in the mornings during the regular workweek. I don't work on Saturday or Sunday (except for very rare exceptions which I share below), and I don't start my workday until 9:00 a.m. Monday to Friday. My planned workday is 9:00 a.m. to 4:00 p.m. Monday to Thursday, and I will work on Fridays and in the evenings if need be.

My Only Exceptions

There are only two situations in which I allow myself to work on a weekend:

1. If I'm attending an event or conference that takes place on a weekend, then of course I am essentially working during that time.
2. When I'm writing a book; this only happens once every couple of years. I find that the process of writing a book requires me to really unplug from any other kind of work and just focus on that for days at a time. I will

50

take time off during the week if I can to write, but I find that my best full-on dedicated writing time is on a weekend. Go figure! (And yes, I get the irony of that in this case.)

Outside of those two exceptions it has literally been years since I worked on a weekend.

#2: Step away from your computer.

If you want to successfully honor your non-working time, you need to step away from your computer. I rarely turn on my computer on the weekend (unless I'm in the mood for some online shopping), and I *never* check my email on the weekends. Repeat – NEVER! Why? Because if I do, I'll be instantly sucked into the vortex of what is going on in my inbox and find myself starting to work.

Here's the kicker: If you start to *think* about work then you are actually working. And the moment you open up your inbox and see those emails in there, your work brain turns on. Then it's hard to turn it off and you are *much* more likely to do some work just to get it out of your head.

You will most likely go through withdrawal when you break your "checking email all the time" habit; because for many of you, it is an addiction. I know it was for me.

I remember when I quit smoking over ten years ago. It took me over two years to quit, and I can tell you why. It's because I spent two years trying to find a way to be able to have just one cigarette here and there instead of just quitting altogether. You can't just take a quick peek at your email on a Saturday morning and then go about your day, trust me.

It did feel very uncomfortable for a while, almost as though my computer was calling me, saying, "Tina, just one small peek won't hurt. You are missing so much! Come on..."

51

Turn your computer off, shut the office door, and even lock it up if need be. ☺

#3: Do not have email delivered to your phone!

This is in the same vein as above, but truly a stand-alone issue in today's world of the smartphone. Don't, for the love of all things holy, have your email delivered automatically to your cell phone, iPad, or other mobile device. There is no better way to get sucked into the vortex of work than to get a "ping" from your cell phone during your non-working time. No one can resist the ping – you will be compelled to check your email just because you know something is there.

If you have clients who call you on your smartphone, you might want to turn off the ringer on the weekends or get *really* good at not answering the phone.

'Nuff said.

#4: Learn how to say NO.

Learn how to say no to the stuff that impinges on your non-working time. If someone asks you on a Friday afternoon to do something that needs to be ready for Monday morning, and you say yes... well then you've essentially set yourself up for a weekend of work.

If you have people-pleasing tendencies at all, which I know many of us do (myself included), then this will be extra tough for you at first. Saying no is actually a muscle that you need to strengthen over time, and it's a key part of taking your time back (and honoring your boundaries, which we'll talk about in the next chapter).

How do you say no to someone? Two simple steps:

1. **Let people know when you are NOT available for work.** This is important in setting the foundation in any new working relationship, and especially important if you haven't done so already in existing working relationships.

   Here's the kicker: If you have already been working on the weekends, your clients and colleagues will come to expect that from you. And they might resist the change at first. They are used to being able to call you on a weekend, or to send you stuff on a Friday afternoon and have it by Monday morning, so respect the fact that it might take a bit of time for them to adjust as well. And if it truly doesn't work for that person and they need someone who is available on the weekends, then you have to decide whether or not that's a client you want to continue to work with.

2. **Then just say no when they ask you to do something on a weekend.** As long as you've set the stage for not working on the weekend and clearly communicated that to your clients and colleagues, then you have every right to say no.

   If someone asks you for something on Friday afternoon, you simply say, "Not a problem, I'll get to it first thing on Monday." If they need it before then you can say, "I won't be able to get it done before I sign off today, so unfortunately I won't be able to meet your deadline. Would it be OK to get it to you by X time instead?"

BEWARE: When you set your non-working hours and let people know about it, you will instantly be tested. You will have everyone emailing you, asking you to do stuff that impinges on your non-working time. You'll have people who never bothered you before on weekends suddenly trying to call you. I don't know why this is, but I've seen it happen time and time again when someone decides to say no to weekends. I believe it's the universe's way of saying, "Hey, are you really serious about this? Let's check it out and see..."

The more you flex your "saying no" muscles, the easier it gets and the better you get at saying no. It will eventually become second nature. I have no problem these days saying no to people, and it rarely even comes up anymore, whereas years back I would have been shaking in my boots!

#5: Have something more compelling to do.

It is a proven scientific fact that nature abhors a vacuum, meaning that if space is created, something will always come in to fill it.

If you are used to working weekends and decide to stop, you need to know what you are going to do instead to fill that time, *and* you need to make sure it is more compelling than your work or you will go back to working.

I believe that some people work too much because they don't have anything more compelling in their lives to fill that time. So if you want to stop working, you need to consider this:

What will you do with your time instead?

Some ideas:

- Spend time with family. Your spouse and/or kids will be thrilled to get this time with you!

- Visit with some friends. When was the last time you had a girls' or guys' night out?

- Take a day trip. What attractions are there in your area that you haven't visited before?

- Go to the spa. Get a massage. Treat yourself to a haircut. Get your nails done.

- Have more sex. Time is often a big reason why people don't.

- Read a book. It's not unusual to find my nose buried in a book during my non-working time (I'm a voracious reader).

- Play a board game. They aren't just for kids! This can be a blast.

- Watch some TV or go see a movie. There are some seriously good shows out there these days in my opinion.

If you feel guilty thinking about doing any of these things, I hereby release you from that guilt. It's not unusual for entrepreneurs (especially women) to feel guilty about not working and taking time to enjoy themselves. If I may be so bold to say it this way: Get over it and have some fun! ☺

Chapter 5
You Teach People How to Treat You
(Setting Boundaries)

I don't watch Dr. Phil these days, but I used to... and one thing I remember him saying over and over again is:

You teach people how to treat you.

This applies in our business lives as much as it does in our personal lives.

I find that many entrepreneurs allow themselves to be treated poorly in business – by their clients, by their team, and by their colleagues. And it sets them up for a business that sucks the life out of them over time.

How do you know if your boundaries are weak? If you ever find yourself saying or thinking things like:

- "I can't believe so-and-so asked me to do this... I hate doing this kind of stuff."

- "I've got so much work to do already and my clients keep giving me more."

- "I told this person that I wouldn't be around today, but they emailed me anyway!"

- "I don't want to work on the weekends, but I feel like I have to in order to get it all done."

- "My client keeps calling me throughout the day. I'm so tired of them calling all the time, but they won't stop!"

- "Why won't my team leave me alone? They keep bugging me all day and I can't get anything else done."

- "I know I shouldn't do this, but I can't say no or they'll be mad at me."

This is a huge part of what leads people to The Entrepreneurial Trap—and ultimately to being overwhelmed, burned-out, and resentful. All of these issues can be solved by one simple thing:

Boundaries.

A boundary is simply a rule or guideline about what is acceptable in your relationships with others and what you will allow (or not!) in the way people behave with you. In other words, it's teaching people how to treat you. ☺

There are two steps to this process:

1. Set 'em.
2. Enforce 'em.

Setting Boundaries

Let's start with step 1, shall we? It's time to DECIDE what your boundaries are (and yes, that word is capitalized for a reason).

This might seem obvious, but **if you don't know how you want people to treat you, they will not treat you the way you want!** In other words, you need to first decide what is acceptable to you in the way that you work and communicate with people in your business.

We already talked about one of the biggest boundaries in the last chapter—time. This is by far the most important boundary to set. There are many more, and I've created the following list of questions to help you decide what your boundaries are regarding your business:

1. What is the best way for someone to get a hold of you?

Phone? Email? Facebook? Twitter DM (direct message)? Skype? Instant Message? Text? What are the acceptable ways for people to communicate with you?

I'm very much an email kind of girl. If someone wants to get a hold of me, that is their best bet. I'm terrible at answering the phone when someone calls me out of the blue, and have been known not to check my voicemail messages for days. All of my phone calls are scheduled ahead of time (with clients or when I'm teaching) and none of my clients have my phone number, nor are they invited to call me "anytime."

I'm not a fan of doing business through Instant Message. Unless there is a compelling reason to do so, I HIGHLY recommend that you don't make yourself available to your team or your clients via Instant Message. It is simply too distracting. Years ago I worked on a team that used Instant Message a lot and, although it was handy at times, it ended up being a giant water cooler on many days and time was wasted. I didn't Instant Message at all for many years until about a year ago when my OBM, Tiffany, talked me into it. We had worked together a long time so I decided it was OK just for her, and it's not overly distracting (I probably bug her more than she bugs me!)

2. What you will do (or not do)

This goes back to your YES! List. What are you willing to do or not do when it comes to your work? You need to be crystal clear on this or you will find yourself doing things that you either:

- hate doing
- don't know how to do
- or don't do well

And none of those options are going to serve you or your clients. Ideally you want to be spending your time on the things that you do best and that serve the growth of your business.

3. Advance notice from your clients

If you are in a service-based business you will want to be clear on what kind of notice you require from a client in order to fulfill an obligation. Your goal is to become proactive in your business, and if you are continually being asked to do things at the last minute, that will never happen.

It doesn't matter if you are a virtual assistant, coach, or personal trainer – you should talk to your clients about how much notice you need for new projects, ongoing work, and appointments.

For example, if you are a virtual assistant, you do not want your clients to continually give you assignments that need to be done today. That will keep you perpetually in reactive mode and force you to work too quickly and not at your usual level of quality just to get it done. If you are a coach, you don't want clients to ask to talk to you "today" or to expect to hear back from you within minutes every time they send you an email.

Most people I know in service-based industries require twenty-four to forty-eight hours' notice for new projects, and in some cases require even more time.

4. Your turn-around time

Going hand-in-hand with the previous point is your turn-around time. How long will it actually take you to do the work? If you are a web designer, how long will it take you to submit a mock-up of a new client's design? If you are a copywriter, how long will it take you to write that sales page?

In order to manage expectations with your clients, you should be crystal clear regarding this boundary. Never assume that a client knows how long something will take, as you will be surprised how often people expect something tomorrow that might actually take a week. And it only puts undue pressure on you and causes them annoyance when there are mismatched expectations.

5. How to handle last-minute stuff and crises

All this being said, there are times when you need to be OK with breaking your boundaries for a legitimate crisis. But you need to be crystal clear about what is a crisis and what is not.

To me a crisis is anything that is connected to money, like a website going down in the middle of a launch or a buy-button that isn't working, preventing customers from completing purchases. Yes, those need to be fixed right away.

Ensure that other people's lack of planning ahead does not become your crisis. If you have clients who are in continual reactive mode and always ask you for things last minute, it may feel like a crisis but is really just poor planning on their part. For example, if they come up with an idea today and say, "I need to get a website up now so I can send an email out tomorrow!" it's not a crisis and you don't have to treat it as such.

Let people know what constitutes a real crisis, and how to get a hold of you if it is one.

6. Eliminate distractions (family, friends, etc.)

Our loved ones can be a HUGE source of distraction if we let them be. Let the people around you—especially those who live in your home—know when they can and cannot disturb you.

Let your friends know that even though you are home, you are working, and that you won't answer the phone when you are working. Have a separate office space in your home, preferably with a door, so that you can shut the door when you are working and others will know that you are not to be disturbed during that time. And if you have young kids, I highly recommend that you get care for them during your working hours.

I believe there is no such thing as working effectively from home when there are kids at home.

After my daughter Samantha was born in 2006, I officially became a work-at-home mom. I was able to juggle the work/family thing for about a year... and then it became abundantly clear that trying to do both at the same time means that neither gets done well. Having Sam home with me while I was trying to get work done was highly frustrating.

I would find myself getting annoyed (and sometimes downright mad) when she would "interrupt" my work. How dare she wake up from her nap early when I'm on the phone! That sounds absurd now, but it is truly what would go through my mind.

When Samantha was about eighteen months old she started going to a day home for the mornings so that I would have some dedicated time to get work done. Lexi was born in 2008, and she stayed home with me for a while (gotta love it when the little ones still have their long naps!), then started going to a day home when she was about eleven months old. Now they are both either in school or at their day home during my regular workweek (Monday to Thursday, 9:00a.m. to 4:00p.m.)

You can't be a good work-at-home mom or dad when you are distracted, and having kids in your home while you are working is highly distracting. The solution? Have someone else take care of your kids during your working hours. Or you might want to do what my friend Pam Slim of EscapeFromCubicleNation.com did and get an office outside of the home. She told me:

> "I worked from home for many years. We always had babysitters for the kids but my office was in the top landing of the house (without a door) and it was tough. The kids would come home from school and want to see me right away regardless of what I was doing. My daughter would grab my leg in the middle of a national radio interview. I started to get annoyed about not having enough time and space for my work, and wasn't relaxed when the kids were around. It became clear that this wasn't fair to them or me, and so in January of 2010 I decided to get an office outside of the home and have never looked back."

For many moms this is a toughie because they thought that working from home would mean being able to spend all day with their kids, right? But it's really a matter of what serves EVERYONE the best. You can't serve your clients when you are distracted. You can't truly be with your kids if you are trying to do work at the same time. And YOU will get exhausted trying to juggle both.

How do you know what boundaries you need to set?

Easy: Pay attention to what you complain about. Do you find yourself saying, "I can't believe so-and-so did X," or "I really wish so-and-so wouldn't do X anymore," or "I'm so tired of doing X"? Our complaints are actually a goldmine in many ways, including setting boundaries.

Enforcing Boundaries

It's one thing to set boundaries; it's entirely another thing to enforce them. Actually setting the boundaries is the easier part; enforcing them can be a whole other ballgame.

As mentioned in the last chapter, you will be tested! As soon as you set a boundary, expect yourself to get many opportunities to enforce that new boundary.

The best way (the only way, really) to enforce a boundary is to learn how to say no. This is a tough one for many entrepreneurs! I've talked to people from start-up to multiple-seven figure businesses who struggle with this. Let's take a closer look at why it can be so hard to say no.

You Are a People Pleaser

This was me for many years. And I believe that being a people pleaser is actually an amazing strength in business. It means you are looking out for someone other than yourself, and I think that's a great gift to give to your clients, team, and colleagues.

But like any gift there can be a dark side, and that's when we say yes to everything out of fear. We say yes because we don't want to let someone down. We say yes because we think we'll look stupid or unprofessional if we say no. We say yes because we hate the thought of someone being angry with us.

In my earlier days of being an OBM I would say yes to pretty much anything a client asked me to do—morning, noon, and night. My biggest motivation was that they wouldn't get angry with me. The thought of having an angry or even just disappointed client was horrible in my mind. I hated confrontation (still do, to be honest) and would do anything to avoid saying no. So I just defaulted to saying yes, even if it meant working 24/7 or doing projects that I shouldn't have been doing.

I remember the first time I stood up to a client and said no. I had planned on taking a few days off and had told this client that I would be away. When I left, everything was done, but knowing they were in the middle of a launch I said I would check in once on a certain day. Off I went on my vacation, and although I was tempted to check in with this client earlier than the agreed-upon day, I did not cave in. When I did check in, they were in panic mode, stressed out and mad at me for not being there when they wanted me to be (even though I had told them about my plans and given them ample notice). I stood my ground, essentially saying, "I told you that I wouldn't be available until now. I'm game to help you with X but I can't promise that I'll be around all weekend." This didn't work for that particular client, and it resulted in the termination of the relationship because I simply wasn't willing to be available when they wanted me to be. It was the first time I truly stood up for myself and, although it was hard, and part of me hated the confrontation, it helped me build my "no muscle," which has served me to this day.

Now I have no problem saying no when something doesn't fit my boundaries. And I rarely (if ever) have anyone angry with me. Go figure!

Saying Yes Fills a Personal Need

This is related to being a people pleaser, with a twist. You might be saying yes to everything because it fills a personal need for you. It could be that you have a need to be needed, or that you love being in situations in which you get to save the day and prove your value.

I remember first learning about this concept from the work of Thomas Leonard, who many (myself included) consider to be the founder of the personal and business coaching industry. Thomas was a pioneer in many ways, and one of my favorite works of his was about needs. He spoke about how our needs drive a lot of our actions, and that if we don't take care of specific needs we will never be able to change our behavior.

This can be some pretty deep stuff, and I'm no psychologist. But I have seen evidence of this in myself and in clients I've worked with over the years. If you find yourself still saying yes to things that you know you want to say no to, explore and evaluate which of your personal needs are not being fulfilled and work on those.

You Don't Want to Miss an Opportunity

This is a really big trap for entrepreneurs—you can't say no because you feel like you are missing out on something. If you say no it might be the opportunity of a lifetime that just passed you by.

I have never found this to be true. And even if my saying no meant that I missed out on something, nine times out of ten the person was willing to work within my boundaries (such as schedule a call at a time that worked for me), or the opportunity came back in a different form (I was invited to speak at someone else's event instead).

Someone recently reached out to me to speak at his event about one of my favorite topics – hiring a virtual team. The event was during the weekend of my daughter's sixth birthday party, and I simply wasn't willing to miss that. Was there a part of me that wanted to say yes? Heck yeah! It was an amazing opportunity to speak to a group of my ideal clients. But a bigger part of me was not willing to miss that time with my daughter, as per my boundaries, so I happily said no.

Be Aware That Saying No Can Change (or End) a Relationship

If you have been saying yes to everyone around you, starting to say no could ultimately end a relationship. It certainly doesn't have to, but you'll want to prepare yourself for that possibility.

For example, if you are in a support role of some kind (such as an Online Business Manager) and your client is used to your being there 24/7 and getting projects done right away, they probably want to keep it that way. They might strongly resist your new boundaries. And even if they initially accept them, you might find that regardless of how often you need to remind them, they still keep pushing your boundaries or getting upset when you say no.

You might have to decide that an old client does not fit your new boundaries, and that you don't want to continue to work with them. And they might decide for you and end the relationship themselves if they are really unhappy with your new boundaries.

This is never fun, and these situations can make it REALLY hard to stick to your boundaries. But remind yourself about why you are doing this. If your boundaries are really important, you need to be OK with letting someone go. Keep in mind that letting someone go usually means that the right fit is just around the corner.

CHAPTER 6
THE FREEDOM MINDSET:
GETTING OUT OF YOUR OWN WAY

It's one thing to know that you want more freedom in your business—it's another to actually create it. The biggest obstacle is your mindset—the way you think. Strive for what I call the *Freedom Mindset*, in which your thoughts support your journey instead of hinder it, and you are able to see possibilities without getting buried in negative self-talk or worry.

This is not easy for most of us! There are all kinds of deeply held beliefs and habits that get in the way when we aim to make changes in our businesses (and our lives), even when we know they are for the better. It's your mindset that makes or breaks you on this journey.

Resistance

When you decide that you want more for your business, your mindset (your subconscious) will try to stop you. Gay Hendricks, author of *The Big Leap*, calls this the Upper Limit Problem:

> "Each of us has an inner thermostat setting that determines how much love, success and creativity we allow ourselves to enjoy. When we exceed our inner thermostat setting [nee when we want more and take steps towards it], we will often do something to sabotage ourselves, causing us to drop back into the old, familiar zone where we feel secure."
> —Page 20, *The Big Leap*

Know that resistance will come up. The key is to be aware of it and to recognize it for what it is. The primary sort of resistance I experience is doubt, and every time I start to do something new it rears its ugly head. For example I've been battling doubt every step of the way in writing this book:

- Who am I to write a book on this topic? I don't have it all figured out. I don't have a seven-figure business. So who is going to pay attention to what I have to say?

- Is my book too short? Should I delay publishing and try to write a longer one?

- What if people think my book is lame? Or worse yet, what if I pour my heart and soul into this book and readers don't connect with it at all?

As you can tell, I didn't let my doubts stop me. And that's the key. Learn to recognize what resistance looks like for you and what you can do to overcome it. There are some amazing books available that can help you with resistance and give

70

justice to this topic in a much better way than I can. Be sure to check out:

- *The Big Leap*, by Gay Hendricks

- *The War of Art*, by Steven Pressfield

- *The Millions Within*, by David Neagle

Fulfillment

How does your business fulfill you? I'm not talking about superficial things like money, number of clients, and such. Those are the obvious measures of a business. I'm talking about how you FEEL about your role in the business, the value you bring to the table, and how you define success.

I've always prided myself on being the smartest person in the room. I remember very clearly deciding in third grade that I was going to get straight As in school, and from that point forward I did. Even though I wasn't aware of it, this became a huge part of how I defined myself in life and in business.

- I was always the one that my friends came to with their problems.

- I was always the one that people wanted to partner with in school because I had the answers (or I would just jump in and do all the work).

- Early in my career I was the one who took on the jobs no one else had done before, because I had a gift for figuring things out.

- For many years my business was based on the fact that I already knew a lot of answers or knew how to quickly find them. (When working as an Online Business Manager, my clients relied on me to have the answers, and I delivered.)

71

I've always known a lot of stuff and it became a bit of a calling card for me. Flash forward to 2009 when I decided to shift my business to a training model, which meant a shift in how work was getting done. For the first time ever it was necessary for me to hire my own help, and at face value I was all for it. (After all, it's what I had been preaching for years!)

But then something happened in my business that made me realize I was no longer the smartest one in the room. In June of 2010,our coach issued us a challenge. He asked us to earn more money that month than we had ever earned before. That is a challenge regardless of timing, but for me in that moment it was a double whammy. We had had some really good months that spring, and I had been planning on taking June off to prepare for a new program and a big launch in July. So I wasn't planning on making much money in June. I was already booked solid to prepare for this new program in July... and yet here was this big challenge.

At first I was angry—how dare he issue this challenge now! This was the worst month to do so! (As if these thing are ever convenient.) Then I decided to go for it, even though I had no idea how we would reach this goal.

The next day Tiffany suggested that we open one of our training programs early and start enrollments in June instead of waiting until August. We came up with the idea of doing a "summer school" session and inviting people to join us early. The only problem was that I literally did not have the time in my calendar to prepare for the upcoming program launch *and* do the enrollment (sales) calls for the new summer session.

Then Tiffany offered to do the enrollment calls for the summer session and take that off my plate. My first reaction was, "No way! That's MY job!" Then I thought about it and decided, "What do we have to lose? She wants to do it so let's go for it." And so she took over those calls.

And guess what? **She was better at those calls than I am.** She did (and still does) a kick-ass job of talking to people about the training program and enrolling them if it's a good fit. The surprising thing was that it really hit me to the core and caused me to question my value."If she is so great at these calls and is going to continue to do them, what value am I bringing to the table?"

Here I was in a situation that should be really exciting—someone else on the team making sales, which means more money for the business, woo hoo!—and feeling badly about it. There was a part of me that wanted to stop it—that wanted to take those calls back because "I should do it; I'm the best here."And then it hit me... this is all part of growth.

As our businesses grow, we need to learn how to let go of certain things and allow others to step into that space.

This caused me to really step back and analyze what value I was bringing to the table."If I'm no longer the smartest one in the room, then what? How do I want my business to fulfill me? It was the first time I realized that I can't do it all, and that I was going to have to change how *I* felt about my own role in my business. I was going to have to change how my business "fed" me.

I'm not going to say that I figured this out overnight. In fact I don't remember the exact moment I was able to let this go. But for a while I was very uncomfortable with it, even though I wasn't going to take those sales calls back from Tiffany – she is better at it then I am, and she loves it!

How Does Your Business Fulfill You?

We are all driven to find fulfillment in our businesses, which can include things like:

- Being the smart one with all the answers (like me!)
- Feeling needed (being the one people turn to)
- Having people like you
- Getting stuff done and saving the day
- Being popular (the one that people want to be around)
- Being the expert or the best
- Having fun and being social
- Being different (doing things that others don't do)

Some questions to consider:

- What do you think you do best in your business? What can you never imagine giving up?

- How does it make you feel to think about giving it up and having someone else do it for you (assuming that they do a great job)?

- What could get in the way of your letting something like that go?

- What would you like people to say about you?

Personal Responsibility

I find responsibility to be a very fascinating topic, and being an entrepreneur challenges your responsibility like few other things can.

There are two sides to responsibility. You either take responsibility for a situation, or **you blame something or someone else for your results.**

Think of a time when you weren't successful. You either owned up to it or you blamed it on something else—the bad economy, or you got sick, or perhaps someone didn't do something they said they would.

I think there is a truth about responsibility that can be a hard pill to swallow: **When you blame someone or something else, you give away your power. And that's a scary thing.**

Being responsible means that you own the good with the bad, the things that worked out with the things that didn't work out. You get to own it all, not just the good stuff.

Have you ever heard the saying that you create your own reality? I couldn't tell you the first time I heard this but it certainly struck home for me. How cool to think that I can have whatever I want in life! That I can become whatever I want to become! That I can accomplish whatever I want to accomplish! If this is true, then it means we are 100 percent responsible for everything in our lives. The good, the bad, and the amazing!

I like to consider my life and business a grand experiment of creating my own reality. When things don't work out the way I thought they would or the way I wanted them to, I aim to look for the lesson rather than the blame. Finding the lesson means I get to keep my power; placing blame means I am giving it away.

Let's say I hired Bob to help me with a project and, although everything seemed like it was on track, he didn't deliver on time. At face value it's easy to say, "Bob screwed up. It's totally his fault." That is placing blame. Instead you might ask yourself:

- "How did I contribute to this situation? Maybe I wasn't clear on my expectations and made assumptions that he understood what I needed and when. Maybe I didn't follow up with him to make sure things were on track. Maybe I wasn't available to him when he had a question."

- "What would I do differently next time?" This is the true lesson, and if you don't explore it, chances are the same issue will show up again and again.

Being 100 percent responsible isn't an easy thing, and so I ask you:

- What are you comfortable being responsible for in your biz?

- What are you uncomfortable being responsible for? (What would you like to blame on someone else?)

- When have you blamed other people or situations when things didn't work out?

Look for situations in which you blame (or are tempted to do so), and you will see where you need to work on responsibility.

Being a Leader

If you have a business, you are a leader (which might make some of you go, "Eek!"). You are a leader in your company (for you and your team) and outside your company (for your clients and community).

Leadership impacts your business in many ways, and many books have been written on this topic. To me leadership boils down to a very simple thing:

Are you a living representation of what you want to accomplish in your business?

In other words, are you exemplifying what it is that your business is about, both for your team and for your clients? Are you practicing what you preach?

I'm not being a leader if I'm teaching everyone to stop working weekends while working on weekends myself. And I shouldn't take a stand on not working weekends and then turn around and expect my team to do so. Leadership comes from having integrity and aligning your actions with what you teach or offer. And it is through responsible leadership that you are able to inspire and lead people in your business.

- What does being a leader mean to you?

- What scares you about being a leader?

- Where do you feel like you do not have integrity in your leadership?

Are You an Ostrich or a Control Freak?

When it comes to running a business, entrepreneurs fall into one of two categories—ostrich or control freak. This is especially important to understand when it comes to dealing with stress in the business. (And growing a business is certainly stressful at times.)

If you are an ostrich, you default to *avoidance* mode— putting your head in the sand and crossing your fingers, hoping that someone else will swoop in and save the day.

Ostriches don't like—or perhaps don't understand—the behind-the-scenes operations of a business. Some of them really hate it. So they rely too much on other people for the answers and to do the work that needs to be done. They hire and blindly trust people on a whim, and assume that whoever they hired is doing things correctly – which isn't always the case. This can lead to a lot of wasted time and money spent on hiring the wrong people, implementing the wrong systems, and having to fix mistakes down the road.

If you are a control freak, you default to-do-it-all-myself mode, in which you keep everything on your plate, rarely delegate, and end up working yourself to exhaustion. A control freak believes that they do it best and that no one else can possibly do the work as well as they can. Although this might be true to a degree, it's a dangerous mindset because they can get caught in the trap of doing the wrong work. A control freak can spend so much time and energy on the behind-the-scenes operations that they don't have time to actually grow their business and deliver their services (per their YES! List). This leads to a lot of frustration, long working hours, and ultimately, burnout.

What you should aim for is something in between an ostrich and a control freak—what I call an *Empowered Entrepreneur*. When you are empowered as a business owner, you:

1. are *aware* of what it takes to run and grow your business (instead of putting your head in the sand)

2. have systems and a team in place that you know can get the job done (instead of trying to do it all yourself)

78

3. own your responsibility for running your business, and won't settle for less than the best for everyone concerned (including yourself!)

Be aware of the boomerang effect. I've seen people go from one extreme to the other and find themselves in a bigger mess than ever. For example, someone who is a control freak may decide they want to let go, and instead of aiming for that middle ground they swing the other way and totally unplug from their business. They hire a team and just leave it to them to run their business, only to find out later that things are a big mess and they have to come in to save the day. Then they swing back to the other extreme again and find themselves right back where they started.

I shiver when I hear a business owner say something like:"I just need to hire the right team and trust them to get the job done."That is blind faith and a seriously dangerous way to run a business.

Control is necessary! Being a control freak is not. As an entrepreneur you need to be in control of your business. You need to have a finger on the pulse of what is going on in your business at all times. You need to be able to access the necessary information to check on the status of projects, clients, and money.

Control and trust are two sides of the same coin, and your *systems* are the bridge between the two for you and your team. With the right systems in place (as we'll discuss in the next chapter) you will be able to let go of the day-to-day work (trust) while still having a finger on the pulse of what is going on in your business (control).

Your Freedom Mindset—Awareness Questions

Awareness is how I avoid getting in my own way. When I'm aware of what might get in my way, what might scare me or stop me, I find it much easier to work through situations.

I invite you to answer the following questions. Spend some time on them and dig deep to see when or how you might get in your own way.

What does freedom in your business mean to you? How does it change your life?

Imagine if you did NOTHING all day and still made oodles of money—how would that feel? Would you feel satisfied?

How are you getting your needs met in your business—being the smart one, feeling needed by others, being in control, feeding off the chaos?

What would you like people to say about you? (Great clue to how your needs are being met in your biz.)

What are you comfortable being responsible for in your biz?

What are you uncomfortable being responsible for?

Where have you laid blame for the results of your business (publicly or privately) in the past?

What does being a leader mean to you?

What scares you about being a leader?

What are you afraid to let go of (delegate or systematize) in your business?

What would make you feel confident about letting something go?

What could happen to make you take something back?

Where would you like to establish high(er) standards in your business?

What could get in the way of establishing and enforcing your standards?

In what situations do you allow your boundaries to be pushed or crossed?

What will it take for you to stand firm in a "no" when your boundaries are being pushed?

Now that you've set your non-working hours, what are you willing to do in order not to work during that time (such as put away your computer on the weekends)?

Where are you taking things personally in your business? How does that keep you from being an Empowered Entrepreneur?

Chapter 7
Systems: Building
the Automation Habit

It's time to shift into the second part of the Automate Your Growth Formula—systems!

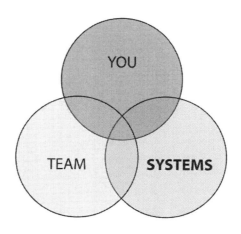

Systems isn't the sexiest topic, right? Many entrepreneurs I know think systems are boring or want to run screaming when they hear the word. But systems are actually the secret key to creating freedom in your business. The stronger your systems, the more you will be freed from the day-to-day running of your business.

Setting Up a Business That Runs Without You

My goal for you is that you set up your business so it can run without you—so you are able to work as much as you would like to work and also do the things you want to do (your YES! List).

For many of you this does not mean that you will work only four hours a week and spend the rest of your time on the beach sipping margaritas. Rather it means that you get to do the work you want to do when you want to do it, and that you take time off when you like—be it weekends or for a full-on vacation—and your business runs without you there.

I believe that most of us would not be satisfied working just a few hours a week.

This is a popular notion for many entrepreneurs, and the topic of much discussion over the years.

You are an entrepreneur, and you started your business for a reason. For many of us that reason was to be able to do work that we love, make a difference in our own way, and make a good living. You enjoy your work (or want to enjoy it again) and would probably be bored if you didn't have your work. I know I would be.

Most people actually don't want to work just a few hours a week and sip margaritas on the beach the rest of the time. What they want to do is spend more of their time doing the work they love—the work that feeds their soul —and less of the work they hate.

Read that again—it's not about not working, it's about doing the work you love.

I believe that as human beings we are meant to work and contribute, and if we stop working (contributing) we lose something in our lives.

Even those I know who have the option to truly work just four hours a week work more than that. They work on new projects and other things besides their primary business—they don't just lie around all day eating bon-bons (although I'm sure they can do that whenever they want to).

If you really want to work just a few hours a week (or not at all), that is something that you earn. It comes after investing time, energy, and effort in your business for a solid period of time – ten to twenty years in many cases. It won't happen because you read a book or bought a program that said you would be able to do so. It happens as a result of seriously investing yourself in a business with the intention of this payoff down the road.

People Are Unreliable, and It's Dangerous to Run a Business Based on People Alone

Many people (myself included!) talk about the importance of hiring a team and getting help in your business. But people alone aren't the answer.

You can hire the best people in the world, but what happens when they are gone? What if they leave your company, get sick, or take some time off for a vacation? What happens to your business when an emergency pops up and they're not available for a period of time? Is your business set up to continue to run without them, or will you and the rest of the team be launched into panic mode trying to figure out what that person was doing and how to do it?

We had a situation earlier this year that unfortunately allowed us to test this. It was February, and we were just three weeks away from the start of one of our major training programs—a week-long intensive training. We were in full-on preparation mode, getting all the final pieces in place, welcoming our new students, getting their materials to them, enrolling a few last-minute attendees, and preparing for the training itself. It was a Thursday afternoon and I got a Skype message from Tiffany that said:"My sister has been killed in a car accident. I have to go be with my family and I don't know how long I'll be away."

I'm sure you can imagine that this was a heartbreaking situation, and as of that moment Tiffany was no longer available to work nor did we know when she would be back. She was 100 percent unavailable in the middle of a pretty busy time in the business.

But because we had been working really hard on our systems and had applied everything I am teaching in this book, it was barely a blip on the radar for me and the team. Because we had worked so hard to centralize our project management, we were able to login to Central Desktop (our virtual office tool of choice), see what Tiffany had on her to-do list, and reassign it to other team members. Because we had worked so hard to document our processes, the other people on the team knew how to do the work that needed to be done instead of scrambling to figure it out on their own. Because we had automated a lot of our procedures, many of the things that needed to be done were already setup and ready to go.

Tiffany was away for almost two weeks, and outside of the obvious sadness for her situation, it was not a stress on me or the rest of the team at all. And Tiffany shared with me later that because she knew we had these systems in place she was able to focus 100 percent on her family rather than having thoughts of her clients in the back of her mind. She knew that we would be fine so she didn't have that worry on top of everything else that was going on. That is the greatest gift that systems can bring—peace of mind.

Systems are the bridge between you and your team. They allow you to create a business that can run regardless of the people involved. They allow you to easily train a new employee or subcontractor, or have someone cover for a colleague while they are away. They allow you to keep a finger on the pulse of projects and what is getting done (or not getting done).

Let's define what a system is:

A system is many parts that work together as a whole to perform a certain task.

When you think about it, systems are already all around us throughout life and business. The way you send out a newsletter is a system. The way you process a payment and the way you welcome a new client are systems. What's important is whether your systems are purposeful (well-thought-out and intentional) or not (making it up as you go each time).

A great example of a system is your morning routine. What does your morning routine look like? Do you have a well-thought-out and intentional start to your morning or do you just fly by the seat of your pants and wing it? One lends itself to a strong start for your day; the other can result in a chaotic and painful start for your day (for instance, you're late out the door getting the kids to school yet again!).

My husband is the ultimate example of a person with a strong morning routine, and I've often joked with him that he has it down to the minute (which he really does). He gets up at the same time everyday, takes a shower, takes the dog for a walk, has breakfast, cleans up the breakfast dishes, and starts his workday. Outside of the occasional blip on the radar (which of course happens with two young girls!) he has a smooth start to every day.

Systems apply to all of life, not just business. And although we are focusing on business, I invite you to consider some of your personal systems as well while you read about systems.

A Proactive Business Needs Systems!

As you know, part of the goal of the lessons in this book is for your business to become a proactive business, and systems play a key part in this goal. They build consistency in effort and results. Strong systems mean that whoever is doing the work will be able to do it the same way as any other person and create the same results. For example, if you have a well-documented system in place for sending out your newsletter, it should happen the same way each time it's sent. If you don't, it probably looks different each time, has an inconsistent feel newsletter to newsletter, and mistakes are made during distribution.

It takes less work to follow a system versus trying to think up a new one each time you perform a task. If you have a well-laid-out system for sending a newsletter, it requires less effort to send that newsletter. If not, you (or a team member) have to think it through each time:"How did we do that last time? I need to go check a past issue. Oh no, I forgot this part and have to go back and fix it...". Having to reinvent the wheel each time you do something is a huge waste of time and energy, and it's costly, especially if you pay your team by the hour.

Systems also allow you to leverage the growth of your business. With strong systems in place you can easily continue your growth, including adding new team members. I know of people whose businesses grew too quickly without systems, only to have everything fall down around them like a house of cards, even to the point of bankruptcy—ouch!

And last but certainly not least, for those of you who are still doing much of the work in your businesses yourselves, until systems are in place you will always be the center of everything. You will always need to either do the work yourself or continually show people how to do it. Tiring!

In other words:

Systems allow you to create a business that functions smoothly, effectively, and freely—**so that you (and your team) don't have to spend all your time putting out fires and trying to keep up.**

Effective Systems

The following diagram illustrates the three key components to having effective systems.

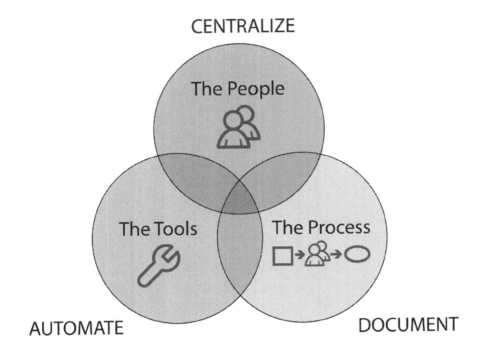

Automate

My definition of *automation* is "no thinking required." It's not just about having everything done through technology (tools), it's about setting up your business so that you and your team spend as little time as possible thinking about:

- what needs to be done
- how to do it

Ideally you should set up a project plan that clearly identifies what needs to be done, who does it, and when. And you should be able to quickly and easily find the plan. Once this is automated (via centralizing and documenting as outlined next), your brain is free to think about the stuff that matters—to be creative and to be focused on delivery of programs and working with clients.

Technology definitely comes into play. As we discuss in the next chapter, there are some amazing tools out there that can help automate many of the things that you and your team are doing.

- Automate ongoing tasks as much as possible. For example, use an online scheduler to coordinate and book appointments rather than having an assistant do the "back and forth to find a time that works" game.

- Automate reminders so you don't have to rely on your memory to think about what needs to be done and you can always see what is coming next.

- Automate your marketing and delivery so it is consistently working for you (more on this in Chapter 9).

Centralize

Before this virtual work-from-home world that many of us now function in, centralizing was simple. You had an office and everyone and everything was in it. You worked side by side with your team and you were able to find files that you needed right there in the office.

In today's business world this is no longer the case. Many of us work virtually, and rarely (if ever!) see each other face to face. This means that many businesses have their materials and information all over the place—in their inboxes, on their computers, maybe written in a notebook. If another member of the team needs something, they have to ask for it and perhaps wait a long time to get it. Two people can have different versions of the same thing, and no one knows which files are the most recent ones.

The goal of centralizing is simple:

Get stuff out of inboxes, computers, notebooks, etc., and into one central location!

Centralizing is all about people—creating a place where you and your team interact throughout the day. This includes:

- Project management–all tasks are listed in one place for all projects

- Online storage–all business files for the team are in one place

- Standard operating procedures (SOP)guide–the how-to guide for you and the team needs to be easily accessible to all (more on this below)

How can you centralize? It starts with getting a virtual office tool that allows you to manage projects, store files, and create your SOP guide in one place – a tool that all members of your team can log into as needed throughout their workday.(We use and love Central Desktop for our virtual office, however there are many more available. See the ET Toolbox at the end of the book for a copy of the Choosing Your Virtual Office Checklist.)

This leads me to what I consider to be the biggest mistake you can make when it comes to running your business: keeping all your to-dos in your head, in a notebook, or in your inbox.

I'll be honest; I did this for years. I kept a lot of the stuff that needed to be done either in my head or in my inbox. You can get away with this to a point, but I guarantee you that it will catch up with you and become a huge source of frustration as your business grows.

When something lives in your head, a notebook, or an inbox, it is a recipe for dropping balls, missing tasks, and making mistakes. It keeps you in reactive mode, always having to think, "What needs to be done next? What about this piece?" Your brain is always plugged in, trying to keep track of it all, like an engine that never stops running (tiring!).

Inboxes get messy. Most people have A LOT of stuff in their inboxes, and trying to keep track of what needs to be done in there can be like trying to find a needle in a haystack, not to mention that the people on your team may be working with many clients and trying to juggle everything from everyone in their own inboxes, too. Yikes! It's no wonder that balls get dropped and stuff gets missed—the system is broken.

How do you fix it? Put in place a virtual office that includes a strong project management tool, something that both you and your team can access anywhere, anytime. And yes, the word *online* is key here. The to-do list in your email software is not the answer because only you can see it.

The primary reason for having a virtual office tool in place is **so you can stop having to constantly think, "What needs to be done? What is coming up next?"** This will suck the life out of you and cause those middle-of-the night moments when you wake up wondering if things have been taken care of.

With a virtual office tool in place, you get to:

- put all the to-dos into the system, complete with due dates and who is taking care of them
- store all essential files that people need to do their work
- forget all about it until you need to take action!

Let me give you an example. When we have a new project, such as the launch of our next Automate Your Growth 90-Day Program, here's what we do:

- Identify what we are aiming to accomplish and the overall strategy – I do this with Tiffany.
- Tiffany then lays out all the steps and to-dos for the entire project.
- Then she plugs ALL those steps into our Central Desktop, complete with due dates and who is doing each step.

The system is set up to send out notifications about new tasks and daily reminders about what is due and what is coming up so everyone on the team is aware of what they need to do and when.

I just sit back and wait for the system to tell me what I need to do next. This has made a HUGE life-changing difference for me. I used to spend a lot of brain power thinking about what needed to be done, when, who was doing it, did it get done, etc. Now I know that the system will remind me when tasks are coming due and when tasks have been completed so I can forget about them until I need to take action. **My project management tool gets to do all the worrying for me—I love that!** ☺

The toughest part is building the habit of using the virtual office tool. It's tough for you as the biz owner and probably for your team as well. It can be hard to break that inbox habit! The biggest consideration in changing your habit is to make sure that someone owns the responsibility of keeping the project management (PM) tool up to date. Ideally this is your Online Business Manager, but if it's you for now, that's totally OK. This person needs to make sure all the to-dos are being put into the PM tool, be a "loving nag" to ensure people are getting stuff done, and make sure tasks are marked as complete along the way so you have an accurate indication of the status of each project.

If you don't have a virtual office tool in place already, it's time. Don't wait until the walls are falling down around you to get it set up. And if they are already falling down, it's definitely time!

Breaking the Inbox Habit

It's one thing to get a virtual office in place; it's another to start using it. It takes time to break the inbox habit. Some of my favorite tips:

- Set your virtual office as the homepage of your browser so it is the first thing you see when you open up your browser each day. This keeps it front of mind. My browser page opens up to the "My Tasks" tab in Central Desktop so I can see what is on my plate for that day.

- Make it the first thing you check in the morning (before email!) and the last thing you check each day before signing off.

- Start sending requests to your team via the virtual office instead of using email. This trains you AND them to use the system.

95

- Ask your team to slap your wrist when you don't use the tool.

Wondering how this can have an impact on your business? Consider this example from Kevin Harris, FAIA, Founder and Principle of Kevin Harris, Architect, LLC

Office communications for many creative professionals can be inefficient, obscure, and frustrating. Our thirty-year-old architectural practice was no different, and all too often our well-intended staff was redrawing good work as a result of a misunderstanding or a misinterpretation of one of my cryptic directives. I found myself wishing my key staff would be able to somehow read my mind. This inefficiency was very expensive, and having to redraw something was demoralizing to everyone.

Our best effort to deal with this was to evolve our practice of using email for task delivery. When we first listened to Tina speaking about her "Leaky Bucket Syndrome" she described our method of using email as the WORST medium for effective project communications. Ouch. That hit home. We knew email wasn't the best way. We weren't in denial but we didn't know what do.

We decided it was time to start centralizing and using a project management tool that we already had but weren't using—Base Camp. Within a week, use of Base Camp for intra-office task management was the new norm. Finally, both staff and principals could readily access where each project was, which tasks were pending, and which tasks were completed. We instantly saw improvements in four key areas:

1. **Transparency**: Before centralizing no one had a grasp on team-member workload. Much project manager time was consumed with tiptoeing around, feeling out one another's potential availability, and determining what each was doing. Tempers would flare when someone fully burdened with work was asked to lighten someone else's load.

   Now every team member can see what the others are working on by project or by person. The frustration and time waste of searching through endless back and forth emails (at best) or truncated emails with more than two people are over. All conversations surrounding any given task stay within the system. It's all there. It's all transparent. All that angst and annoyance and posturing has been eliminated. Gone. Removing the emotion from the process of documenting, delegating, and managing tasks saves all of that energy for the task itself. Transparency rocks.

2. **Accountability**: The transparency of the system leads directly to ease of accountability. Tasks are assigned and given dates. Each team member can look anytime—and from anywhere with Internet service—and know what is on their plate. Team members are empowered to have objective discussions about workload realignment. When project managers delegate tasks, Base Camp tracks the tasks and the delegation. As the principal of the firm, it's all there for me to see when I do a routine check. I am likewise empowered to reassign tasks or deadlines should priorities shift. Once again, a lot of emotion is saved. No angst, worry, or nagging.

3. **Clarity**: As an architecture firm, our most proficient communication method is graphic and not verbal. So another downside of our creatively assigning tasks was interpreting the "fuzzy" factor of written or verbal instructions. I would give a verbal instruction and the staff member would complete what they thought I meant. Way too often this method resulted in a disconnect between what I had intended and what the team member initially provided, necessitating a "redraw."

Now that tasks are scribed into Base Camp, there is an opportunity for clarity long before a "failed" (from my perspective) completion. Once assigned, our team members document their understanding of the objective and outcome. I can see what the team member entered, and if the stated outcome was not quite what I intended I can write a clarifying note before they start the work. Happy boss, happy staffer, happy client. WIN!

4. **Efficiency**: Now that we've captured tasks through the duration of a given project, we have created (without any additional effort) a knowledge base of activities related to how our firm delivers projects. This becomes a ready reference to use in planning tasks for subsequent projects. We are optimistic that over time this knowledge base will give us a more transparent, clear, accountable, and efficient way to deliver our projects.

Through centralizing our tasks, the firm has taken a giant leap forward towards focusing our creative energies on DESIGN and not on endlessly reinventing a process for delivering it!

Document

One of the biggest excuses I hear from business owners when it comes to hiring a team and getting tasks off their plate is:

"No one does it as well as I do."

It could very well be true that people on your team never do something in exactly the same way you would. But when you purposely put good systems in place—in particular a strong set of documented processes in your SOP guide—you can bring them as close as possible to "being you."

For example, if there is a very particular way you like to see a sales page setup, create a template with a list of instructions so that anyone else can create a page just the way you like it. This is as close to cloning yourself as you can come. If you take the time to document a process and clearly lay out the steps for doing it, this allows others to do it as well as you, which means you can (finally!) get things off your plate and know that your team will do them right.

In some cases you just need to be able to let go. Sometimes people on your team will do something differently than you would, but that doesn't mean it's wrong. **As long as the same result is achieved, their way can be just as effective.**

For example, one of the things I've given to my team is to write the welcome letter that gets sent to people when they join a program. Do they write the letter in exactly the way I would? No. But so long as the key information is in there, it doesn't matter. As long as the person receiving the letter has what they need, it's a good letter.

I've been working with my team for over three years, and I very purposely continue to let go of more and more things. To this day there are times when I see a member of my team doing something and think, "That's not the way I would do it... it should be like this." And then I have to pause and ask myself a couple of questions:

- Can I create a documented process so someone else can do it my way?

- If their way achieves the same result, can I just let this go?

Often I simply need to let it go, even when it feels tough, because I know I'm going overboard with the control freak in me.

Set standards, templates, and guidelines for your business. That is a key part of creating systems. There will always be a bit of a grey area where your team puts their own touches into the mix, so learn to appreciate those touches and move on to more important things.

One of the biggest mistakes I see entrepreneurs making is **not documenting their "how-tos" and having to reinvent the wheel every time something needs to be done.**

Consider this scenario: You are launching a new program and want to do a free training call as part of the promotion. You ask your team to set everything up for you just like last time.

- Your team isn't totally clear on what you want, so they come back and ask, "What do you mean like last time? Where can I find that information?"

100

- You feel a bit annoyed and reply, "You know, the call we did back in March. I want to do the same thing this time around!"
- They don't want to keep bugging you, so they go ahead and setup everything based on what they think you want. They send it to you saying, "Done!" and lo and behold, it isn't at all what you were looking for.
- At this point you are either a) so frustrated that you decide to do it all yourself just to get it done right, or b) wonder what the heck is wrong with your team and why this keeps happening.

This is a pretty common occurrence and it affects both sides:

- You are frustrated because you don't have the time and energy to hold your team's hand every time you want something done.
- Your team is frustrated because they weren't 100 percent clear on what you wanted, made their best guess, and thought they were on the right track, only to find out that it wasn't what you wanted at all.

Everyone is wasting time and energy going back and forth trying to figure this out and get it right, not to mention that you are paying your team to do double the work!

The answer?

Document All Your Key Processes!

Create a list of step-by-step instructions for all the things you know will need to be done more than once, such as setting up a teleclass series, sending out your ezine, enrolling new clients, etc.

This is called a standard operating procedures (SOP) guide—a very corporate sounding term—and YES, every business needs one, even yours. ☺

An SOP guide is important for a few reasons:

- **No more wasting time, energy, and money.** Once a process is documented, ANYONE can step in and follow the steps as needed in the future. This is especially awesome when bringing a new team member on board.
- **It provides consistency in your brand.** You have a certain way of doing things and want to be sure that is reflected in your business consistently.
- **The value of your business is greatly increased if all the systems are in place and documented.** Even if you don't plan to sell your business, an SOP guide is part of a strong foundation to grow on, to continue to make more money, and to keep your sanity.

How do you know when to document something? If you (or your team members) will need to do something more than once, there should be a *documented* system for it. As I'm sure you can imagine, this means there is a lot of documenting to come!

How Do You Tackle Creating an SOP Guide?

First, I want to acknowledge that creating an SOP guide is not the most exciting thing in the world, which is exactly why many businesses don't have one (or only have part of one).It isn't my ideal way to spend a day either, but it definitely needs to be done.

It's like exercise—at first it's not fun. You have to drag yourself out of bed early to make it to the gym when you really don't want to. But you do it anyway because you know the payoff is worth it. Although you may never *love* working out, you get to the point at which it becomes part of your day and it's no longer such a drag.

SOP guides are part of a healthy workout for your business. So to break it down a bit:

- **Who creates the SOP guide?** Whoever is doing the work and knows the process. If you have been doing most of the work yourself to date, then it's you. If you have a VA (or two) who has been doing the work, get them to help (and yes, you pay them for this time).This requires a measure of discipline on both sides – you need to demand that they do it as part of their role, and they need to set aside the time to actually do it.
- **When to start?** Now! The best way to create your SOP guide is "as you go." You and/or your team can start documenting things as they come up. Don't try to do it all at once and make it a big project. That's too stressful and it's not necessary.
- **What is the format?** Your SOP guide needs to live online in a place that is accessible to everyone on the team so it's easy to update. We use the "wiki" feature in Central Desktop to manage our SOP guide. It can be written, audio, video, or a combination thereof.

If you start today, in a few short weeks you will be well on your way to having an effective SOP guide in place and living happily in your virtual office for all to see.

Systems creation needs to be a part of the ongoing fabric of your business. It's not a one-time thing—it's a journey, not a destination. Build the habit of creating or improving systems in your business on a regular basis. Yes, it seems like a lot of work upfront, which can be a turn-off for people. But I assure you that once you have your key systems in place, they are very easy to maintain.

I love the following quotes from the book *Work the System*, by Sam Carpenter:

- "We are not fire killers, we are fire prevention specialists. We don't manage problems; we work on system enhancement and system maintenance in order to prevent problems from happening in the first place."

- "Problems are gifts that inspire us to action. A problem prompts the act of creating or improving a system or procedure."

The goal of system creation is simple: When a problem occurs, look for a system to prevent it from happening again. Then over time you will have fewer problems and crises that pop up in your business. Dreamy, right?

CHAPTER 8
MY TOP TEN BUSINESS SYSTEMS

Now it's time to dig into the specific systems to create in your business. The specifics of how you apply these systems are different from business to business, but we all need them. Here are the top ten business systems that are must-haves for every business:

1. Backup systems
2. Money systems
3. Scheduling systems
4. Communication systems
5. Metrics systems
6. Marketing systems
7. Relationship systems
8. Sales systems
9. Delivery systems
10. Business foundation systems

These are the ten systems that I teach in my Automate Your Growth 90-Day Program, and although I can't give you all the specifics for each within the scope of this book, I can provide the basics of each.

Let's dive into each of them, shall we? (I've provided a list of my recommended tools at the end of this book in the Appendices so you can find specific information and links for everything mentioned below.)

1. Backup Systems

My husband used to own an IT business, and their tagline was: Lose your data, lose your business.

Your files are your business, and if they aren't being backed up properly, you are at risk of losing your business. Think about what you would do if your computer were suddenly wiped out and you had no backups? Makes me shiver to think about it.

There is a reason this is first on the list, and that is because I know that many of you are still not backing up files like you need to be. And I am here to give you a loving slap on the wrist!

Set up automated backup for all the files on your computer. This needs to run automatically, updating your files on a regular basis—ideally each day. This does NOT mean backing up to an external hard drive that sits on your desk. Why? Two reasons:

1. You have to remember to do an external hard-drive backup, and if you need to remember to do it, chances are you won't do it on a regular basis.

2. What happens if you have a break-in and all your equipment is stolen? Or there is a flood or fire and

your equipment is ruined? You will lose both your computer *and the backup.*

I had a client who was backing up to his external hard drive, and was very religious about it. Then the unthinkable happened—both his computer and external hard drive failed at the same time, and EVERYTHING he had ever created was on there (years of coaching and training curriculum he had created). He took it to a computer professional who was thankfully able to recover the information—at a price of $5,000—which my client was happy to pay given the alternative!

I use and recommend Dropbox for backing up your files. It will automatically backup your files throughout the day – as soon as you close a file, it's backed up within minutes, and I love that! It doesn't affect the performance of your computer at all, like other systems that slow down or hang up your computer when they are running a backup. And because it backs up your files to the cloud (online), you are easily able to access files when travelling and share files with other people on your team.

Centralize all your team files. No one on your team should have any of your company files stored on their own computer. Make sure that you upload all your company files to your virtual office and that your team works with those files directly (vs. keeping copies on their computer).There's nothing worse than losing the latest version of a file because a team member had it on their computer and didn't back it up!

Get backup copies of your websites and databases. If you are using a reputable website hosting company, they will create their own backups of your websites and should be able to restore files if something happens. When my main website was hacked a few years ago and replaced with a picture of a scary clown (and clowns scare me!), we were able to have my hosting company go back a few days and restore my site from that previous version. Phew!

That being said, I think it's a good practice to also have someone on your team do a backup of all of your websites and any associated databases, such as the SQL file of a Wordpress site, just in case. One of my VAs does this for me on a monthly basis. We keep all of these files in our Amazon S3 account, which is where we store large files (such as website files) for a very low price.

Backup your people. What happens when a team member goes on vacation or becomes ill? Who is their backup? Your SOP guide includes procedures for the backup of tasks and responsibilities when someone is away, and it is good practice to determine ahead of time who will cover for each member of the team when they are away.

2. Money Systems

If you aren't consciously taking care of your money, your business will struggle. As entrepreneurs we know that money is important, and we want to make sure that the flow of money is as smooth as possible from buy button to bank account.

How do you process payments? Today there is no excuse not to be accepting some form of automated payment in your business. It might be as simple as accepting PayPal, or you might have a merchant account and an ecommerce (shopping cart) system in place that allows you to process payments.

I don't know about you, but I can't remember the last time I was asked to write a check, be it for business or personal. And when I am asked to write a check, quite honestly it annoys me and I may decide that I don't want to do business with that person or company again. Many larger companies still accept checks as standard practice, but if you work with individuals and/or small companies, I invite you to consider retiring the check.

Accepting electronic payments is especially important when you have clients who pay you on a regular basis. You want a system that allows you to process payments automatically, be it once a month for a regular client or over a period of time for a payment plan. For example, if you have a client who is paying for something over a period of three months, you want to be able to setup the payment to process three times and not have to think about it again unless a payment is declined. You want to be confident that the money will end up in your bank account.

We use Infusionsoft as our ecommerce system to process all of our payments, together with Moneris for our merchant account (which is for Canadians).

Tracking Payments

Do you have a system in place to track and follow up on declined payments from your customers? If not, set one up today. I've heard too many horror stories about business owners who sold X only to find out months down the road that the person hadn't paid due to a declined credit card (or some other payment issue).I've even heard that such a situation resulted in thousands or tens of thousands of dollars of lost income. Yikes!

It is simply bad business not to track payments, not to mention heartbreaking – especially if the timing is such that it's too late to appropriately collect the money. Plan for the following:

- **Put someone in charge of declines**. Make it their responsibility to follow up on overdue payments and bring them to your attention if need be.

- **A spreadsheet to keep track of all declines** or overdue payments so you can see at a glance what is going on (ours lives in Central Desktop).

- **Have your declined payment monitor run a "declines report" at least once a week** from your shopping cart system and record the declines on the spreadsheet (we do this on Fridays).

- **That person should follow up with the client to arrange for payment**. We start with an email (using our template), then follow up a few days later with another email if need be, and then a phone call if there is still no response. Then the matter is escalated to me as the business owner.

Consider what your standards will be for this process. For example, if someone owes a payment of $50 or less and doesn't respond after two emails and a phone call, is it worth it to keep chasing them down? Probably not, as you could spend more money chasing them down than their payment is worth.

The good news is that nine times out of ten people are willing to pay—it's simply a matter of following up with them. Easy peasy.

Cash flow is another area in which you can get yourself into trouble if you aren't careful. Cash flow is simply tracking the flow of money coming in and going out of your business. You need to be able to plan for and balance this flow of money so you don't find yourself in a bind. For example, someone may make a big sale, get all excited, and spend that money right away... only to find that the payment for that big sale is being made in six installments over a period of six months. They've spent money that hasn't been received yet. When you are clear on the timing of the money coming into your bank account (not just the sales amount) and your budget, you should be able to balance the flow of money so that it doesn't cause issues.

And of course you need a good bookkeeper and tax accountant. Your bookkeeper will keep track of all of your finances in a system like QuickBooks (which is what I use). And your accountant will help you plan for taxes and prepare your year-end books each year. A good accountant will also advise you about tax savings strategies for your business.

3. Scheduling Systems

There are lots of things going on in a business day to day, and it can be hard to keep track of what is happening and when. Big problems are caused by leaks in the scheduling systems at many businesses!

How do you book your appointments? The day I discovered Time Trade was a hallelujah day for me. Time Trade is the online scheduling system I use to book appointments with my clients, prospects, and business colleagues. I hated doing the "back and forth email dance" to try to find a time that worked for both parties—so frustrating! With a tool like Time Trade, I just send people a link to my schedule, which allows them to choose from predefined times that I have available. Time Trade syncs with both my Google Calendar and my Outlook Calendar, so I can always see what I have on my schedule. (Yes, I'm still an Outlook girl. ☺)

Your promotional calendar is another biggie. What are you promoting and when? If you have implemented your 3 Steps Ahead Strategy, the next step is to determine the dates for your promotion. Then enter them on your calendar so you can see at a glance what is coming up. This includes promotions that you have promised to do for others as part of joint venture relationships.

Create a publishing calendar, so you can see specifically what information you are sending out on what dates. This is especially important if you have a lot going on and don't want to overload your schedule. A publishing calendar allows you to plan ahead and helps you say yes or no to other opportunities as they come up. It's not unusual for me to have a brilliant idea (ahem) and ask Tiffany, "Can we do this on X date?" First thing she does is look at the promotional and publishing calendar to see if there is space. If there is she might say yes. If not, she'll let me down easy.

Last but not least is your events calendar. We do all kinds of classes and training programs, and it is essential that we have a centralized calendar for me and the team to see what is going on. We use the calendar in Central Desktop, and include all the details for a training program on the calendar so we have easy access to the information we need when we need it.

4. Communication Systems

How do people communicate within and outside of your company? We live in a world of overload, and it is really important that you give your communication systems the attention they need. Consider what works best for you and your team, but also what works best for your clients.

Various ways you can communicate:

☐ **Email, but of course!** Start communicating with your team via your virtual office as much as possible (wink wink). However, most clients and prospects want to be able to reach you via email. It is best to have one support@ or help@ email address for clients and prospective clients to use. Ensure that everyone on your team has their own email address under your domain. You do not want them using their personal email addresses when working on behalf of your company. Not only does that look unprofessional, but it means you don't have access to their email if they are away for any reason.

☐ **How can people reach you by phone?** I highly recommend that you get a toll-free number for your public phone number. This is very easy to do. I got mine years ago via Virtual PBX. Depending on how many phone calls you receive, determine whether it's best that phone calls be answered live or go straight to voicemail. We get maybe one or two calls a week at the most, so all of our calls to the toll-free number go straight to voicemail. We then get an email notification about the message and someone on the team returns the call right away. This makes much more sense than having someone available to answer a phone that rings only twice a week. But of course, if you get a lot of calls you will want someone to answer live!

Outside of your weekly meetings you may not need to talk to your team live very often. I think I've called Tiffany maybe once or twice in the two-plus years we've worked together. That being said, you do want to have the phone numbers of your key team players just in case, and with the intention of honoring their boundaries, of course!

☐ **Instant Message—yea or nay?** This is something I would consider using only for internal communications, and as I've already shared, you will want to be careful who you connect to via Instant Message. It can be highly distracting and can lead to a lot of water-cooler talk if you aren't careful. I would never give Instant Message access to a client or prospect.

☐ **Social media is a biggie these days.** People can reach out to you by posting comments on your blog, Twitter, Facebook, and such, so you need to make sure you will be notified about these messages. I remember years ago finding a post on my blog that someone had written a month before asking a question about a program of ours, but I didn't know it was there! Needless to say, we lost the sale because we didn't reply right away. We now have the blog setup to send an email notification each time someone posts a comment so we can respond.

Customer Service

Part of communications is ensuring that you have a strong customer service system setup and that you take care of answering questions before and after a sale. I won't get into great detail regarding customer service, but I do want to point out some key decisions to be made:

☐ Where will customer service (CS) requests go? Make sure you centralize all of your CS emails rather than having them go to someone's individual inbox. We use Zendesk to manage all of our CS emails, but if you don't have a lot of CS emails, you may want to use something as simple as a Gmail account. So long as you and others on the team can access it in one spot, it's all good.

☐ Who is responsible for answering CS requests? Have one person on the team responsible for ensuring that CS requests are answered. This means they either answer them to the best of their ability, or they pass them along to the right person when appropriate (and they still check in to make sure they have been answered). Our VA Ashley "owns" our Zendesk account and is in there throughout the day to respond to all of our CS requests.

☐ How quickly should you respond to requests? You will want to set a standard here –twenty-four hours or less is ideal. The bottom line is that the quicker you are, the better. Replying quickly can have a huge impact. It's amazing how slow some companies are at replying to CS requests, and that is not good business!

☐ Create templates for responding to common requests so that the CS person can just paste in standard replies and avoid typing the same thing over and over again.

5. Metrics Systems

Metrics is a boring word for a very exciting thing: watching your business grow! Put simply, metrics is tracking your numbers (sales, leads, promotions, etc.) so you can truly see what is going on in your business. There is no way to know how well you are doing (or not) unless you are tracking and reviewing your metrics on a regular basis. Track things like:

- People numbers–prospects and clients

- Sales–products and services

- Broadcasts–open rates and click throughs

- Promotional stats–conversions

- Social media–activity and volume

- Website traffic

- Your goals and your targets

- Changes and trends in all of the above

I recommend setting up a spreadsheet and tracking your metrics weekly. This is something that can be done quite easily by an assistant once the initial spreadsheet is setup. Our metrics spreadsheet lives in our Central Desktop account, and we have someone on the team update it every Monday morning.

6. Marketing Systems

The heart of marketing is how people find your business and how they are exposed to what your business offers. It's all about lead generation—or building a list of prospects.

The best strategy varies greatly from business to business, and can include things like:

- Online traffic and search engine optimization (SEO)

- Social media and blogging

- Affiliate (joint venture) marketing

- Article marketing

- Advertising

- Publicity and public relations (PR)

- Speaking (live or virtual)

To dig into marketing systems would take an entire book in and of itself, so I won't go into great depth here. What I do want you to consider is:

- What are you currently doing to market your business? What is working and what is not working?

- Have you documented your best marketing strategies?

- What can you do to automate your marketing strategies as much as possible?

For example, if you know that social media is a great marketing strategy for your business, ensure that you have setup a system to post your ezine article (or video) each week via the various social media channels. Ensure that your ezine article is always posted to your blog, and that notifications are also posted to Twitter, Facebook, LinkedIn, etc. This can be automated using various plugins for your blogsite that will blast out notifications each time you create a new blog post.

7. Relationship Systems

How do you build relationships with people once they are on your list? How do you build the "know, like, and trust factor" so they will want to buy something from you when it makes sense for them to do so?

Focus on providing value and giving people information they can use right away instead of just trying to sell them stuff. There are a few ways to do this:

- **Send out a regular ezine or newsletter.** It can be weekly (the best choice!) or once a month. The key is to commit to whatever timeline works for you.

  Create an exciting ezine template and document the process for sending out the ezine. Ideally you will create only the *content* for the ezine each week or month, and someone on your team will use the template to complete the job.

- **Social media can be a huge relationship builder.** The key is to find a strategy that allows you to make connections but doesn't take a lot of time from your day. My friend Lena West, social media expert and creator of Influence Expansion, recommends that you schedule two days a week as "connection days." Instead of being on social media all day everyday (as many of us think we need to be), you pick two days a week to be online and interacting. This gives you the opportunity to connect without taking up too much of your time. Love it!

- **Follow-up strategies:** What happens after someone joins your list? This is one of my FAVORITE topics, and I've dedicated the entire next chapter to what I consider to be one of the most underutilized and yet highly effective ways to automate the marketing process and build relationships.

8. Sales Systems

When a lead becomes serious about making a purchase, they shift from your marketing systems to your sales systems. This includes everything from having a sales conversation through to their actually buying something from you.

When it comes to your sales systems you want to consider two things:

1. How does a prospect move into the sales system? Depending on your business and what you offer, this usually occurs online via a sales page or as the result of a live in-person conversation (a sales call).Either way, consider your sales strategy, and, as always, be sure you document and automate as much of the sales process as possible.

2. Follow-up is key! As detailed in the next chapter, I've read many statistics that prove that the majority of prospects don't buy until after the fifth contact with you. So continue to follow up with people on a regular basis or you might miss out on a lot of opportunity!

   Follow-up is easily automated using tools such as Infusionsoft. We help a lot of our clients setup Infusionsoft so that once they make a connection they can automatically follow up with prospects and no one slips through the cracks. Dreamy!

9. Delivery Systems

How do you deliver your products and/or services? Delivery systems vary greatly from business to business depending on what you offer. And there are many ways in today's world to automate the delivery of your products and services.

For example, if you have a tangible product such as a book, you can automate fulfillment of each order. Instead of receiving an order and having someone manually process, pack, and ship it, you can use the services of a company like Vervante which can do all of this for you. Once an order is placed via your ecommerce system, Vervante receives a notification and automatically produces, prints, and ships your product to your client. All you need to do is... well, nothing!—once it is setup, of course.

Be sure to automate your welcome process. We live in the age of instant gratification, and when someone makes a purchase they expect to have instant access to it. How are you welcoming new clients when they make a purchase? Here are some ideas:

- When someone purchases a shippable product, send them an instant confirmation that it is being shipped. Give them access to an online or digital confirmation document right away if possible.
- When someone purchases a digital or online product, be sure to give them access to it right away. Take them to a download page or send them a link via email. Do not send them an email that says, "We will provide access to your purchase within twenty-four hours." There is no reason to delay delivery of an online or digital product with the tools we have available to us today.
- If you offer a membership, send clients directly to a login page as soon as they purchase. Let them choose their own login username, password, and/or code (ideally) and give them information that will help them make the best use of the membership site right away such as a new-member tour video.
- When someone purchases a high-end package from you such as a coaching or implementation package, send them all the details they need right away. Let them know what is included with their package and how they can book their first session.
- Regardless of what they purchase, I think it's a really nice touch to give people a phone call whenever possible, especially for high-end purchases. I can only

120

think of one time in the past few years when someone called me after I made a purchase, and it was a nice treat!

Business Foundation Systems

If you take your business seriously, you need to consider your foundation, including:

- Legal support
- Insurance
- Financial support
- Tax support

These are the official requirements of running a business, and many entrepreneurs don't have all the necessary pieces in place (or they have the wrong pieces in place, which can be even worse!).

These things are not fun to put in place, and in some cases they're downright scary. This is why I am thrilled with and highly recommend Alexis Martin Neely's LIFT Foundation System. Alexis is a lawyer and entrepreneur, and she has seen firsthand the ramifications of not having a strong foundation in place. Her LIFT program is designed to take you step by step through the process for your business. And the best part? You only have to do it once. ☺

You can check out many of the resources I've mentioned in this chapter via this link: www.TinaRecommends.com

CHAPTER 9
YOUR AUTOMATED MARKETING MAP

There are many different ways to automate your marketing, but I want to focus on one that I believe is the most underused marketing strategy and yet can have a really big impact on your bottom line.

Let me start this discussion with some scary statistics that I first read in the book *Conquer the Chaos*, by Clate Mask and Scott Martineau. **When do people buy? In other words, how often does someone need to hear from you before they decide to make a purchase?**

- 2% of sales close on the 1st call

- 3% of sales close on the 2nd call

- 4% of sales close on the 3rd call

- 10% of sales close on the 4th call

- 81% of sales close after the 5th call

When do most businesses stop following up with prospects?

- 48% quit after the 1st call

- 24% quit after the 2nd call

- 12% quit after the 3rd call

- 6% quit after the 4th call

- 10% do 5 or more calls

Put simply...

10% of businesses get 81% of the sales out there.

I've since seen this same statistic over and again, in some cases with slightly different numbers, but the bottom line remains the same: Most businesses do not follow up, which means that the few that do are getting most of the sales.

So the question is: Do you want to be one of the 10 percent getting those sales? (I'm sure it's an obvious yes.)It's not as hard as you might think when you employ a great automated follow-up marketing strategy that leads your prospects to a buying decision with minimal effort from you or your team.

What happens after someone becomes a prospect—after they join your list or give you their business card?

If you are like the 90 percent from the statistics above, chances are not much. They might get an email from you or maybe be added to your ezine list, but that's it. (And just to be clear, I'm not shaking my finger at you—I was guilty of this for far too long.) This is like inviting someone into your home and just leaving them in the foyer. They know there is some cool stuff in your home, but no one has invited them in... so they just stand there (and eventually leave).

Engage with your prospects while they are "hot"!People are the most interested in what you have to offer right when they first take action. When they visit your website and sign up for your freebie, there is a prime moment in time when you need to engage with them and give them more. You need to invite them further into your home.

A good follow-up strategy takes people on a journey through your offerings based on their interests. The best strategies don't employ a one-size-fits-all approach; rather they are able to respond to people based on who they are and the action they took. When someone clicks on a link in your email about a certain topic, you should continue to email them on that topic and get specific instead of sending generic information. And yes, you will need the right technology in order to truly automate this process. (More on that a bit later.)

Let me tell you about the automated marketing map we have created for our Online Business Manager website. People come to our site, www.OnlineBusinessManager.com, where they are invited to receive a free report. After they download the free report, they are taken to a page that invites them to take a readiness quiz for hiring or becoming an OBM. Let's follow the rest of the journey of someone who wants to become an OBM:

- They take the quiz and score somewhere in three different levels (0 to 40, 40 to 70, 70 to 100). Their score lets us know what they are ready for and determines their next steps.

  o If they score 0 to 40, they aren't quite ready to become an OBM, so we put them into our Book Purchase map, which leads them to purchasing the *Becoming an OBM* book—a good next step for a person at this level.

  o If they score higher, they are much more likely to be ready to become an OBM, and are put into the OBM Certification map, which leads them to information about our training programs and how to apply.

- We can tell whether or not they take action, and we follow up with them if they choose not to. For example, we send them an email saying, "I see that you haven't purchased the book yet. Is there a question I can answer for you?"

- Regardless of their current purchase actions, they are put on our OBM Newsletter list and receive information from us on a weekly basis.

During all of this we are building the "know, like, trust factor" with our prospects. The goal is to have them buy (but of course!), but we keep the focus on delivering value at each step along the way. They enjoy the time they spend in our home, getting to know us and everything we have to offer so they can ultimately feel good about making a purchase when they are ready.

Why don't people follow up?

Here are some of the common reasons why you might not follow up properly and end up being one of the 90 percent:

1. **You forget**. If you don't have a good system in place to remind you to follow up with someone, you might simply forget to do so.

2. **You focus on hot leads and forget about following up with others.** It can be really easy to get caught up in the newest people in your network and forget about the other people who have been around longer and might be ready to buy now.

3. **You get distracted by other stuff going on in the business and follow-up falls to the bottom of the list.** I always think of Steven Covey's book *The 7 Habits of Highly Effective People*, and in particular Habit 3: Put First Things First. In his Time Management Matrix he talks about how things are Urgent/Not Urgent and Important/Not Important. Follow-up falls into the category of being Important but Not Urgent. It's so much easier to focus on what's calling for our attention NOW! instead of the things that are truly important to the success of our businesses. (Getting into proactive mode helps here as well.)

4. **You don't know how.** You need to be clear on your strategy and exactly what you need to do in order to take action.

5. **You think the prospect will call back.** This is a huge misconception. "Oh, if they are really interested they will call back." They might have misplaced your information or forgotten your

website. Or if they're like me, they would like to call back but only think about it at inopportune times like the middle of the night. I'm in the market for some landscaping work right now, and let me tell you, if someone called me and asked, "Do you need some help?" I would probably hire them on the spot for the simple reason that they called me and I didn't have to remember to call them.

6. **You don't want to be pushy.** Permission-based marketing is never pushy. This person has asked to get information from you and they expect to hear from you. Permission-based marketing also means that they can opt-out of any marketing efforts if they decide they are no longer interested. Yes, you can go overboard here, but most people default to going "under board" and not reaching out enough.

7. **You don't realize the potential impact follow-up can have on your business.** Review that statistic above again, and that should change your mind. ☺

Strategy for the Automated Marketing Map

So let's dig into some nitty gritty here, shall we? Here is my step-by-step process for creating your own automated marketing map. This is the exact process I use with my clients when we work one-to-one and map out their strategy. At the end of this process you will have your own map or flowchart that clearly identifies what action you want a prospect to take (your end goal) and how you will get there.

There is some work involved in setting up this map, but it is a front-loaded process. If you are willing to put some time, energy, and effort into creating your automated marketing map, it will "do the work" for many years to come!

You may want to create more than one map for different areas of your business, especially if you offer a variety of products or services. For the sake of simplicity, I invite you to pick just one area of your business for now and work its map through to completion. Then come back to create the other maps you need.

Step #1: Take Inventory

Make a list of everything you offer in your business, including:

- Freebies–often called irresistible free offers (IFOs).Your freebie is whatever you are offering on your website to entice people to join your list. It could be a five-part ecourse or a free CD that you ship out to them.

  (Don't forget teleclasses, webinars,and other free classes you offered in the past that people might still be signing up for! People still opt in to classes I offered a year ago.)
- Low-priced items–books, workbooks, classes
- Mid-priced items–group coaching, trainings, events
- High-priced items–one-to-one work, consulting, coaching, VIP programs

Step #2: Sort Your Offers

Now that you have your list, sort them into one of two categories:

1. **Anytime Offers**–these are things that people can buy or access at anytime, for example, your freebies, services, or a book. These are the best ones to plug into your automated marketing strategy, as they are always available.

2. **Time-specific Offers**–these are only available for purchase at certain times, for example a live training program that starts on a specific date. These will not be plugged into your automated marketing strategy, and are instead sold via your ezine, launches, and timed promotions.

Gather up your list of Anytime Offers for the next steps.

Step #3: Determine Your Goal

What *ultimate* action do you want someone to take when they engage with you? What is the goal of your automated marketing map? For many this includes something like:

- Make a purchase–online (by clicking a buy button) or in person (via phone or a retail store). This usually applies to low-priced items that are easily saleable online or via an automated marketing process.
- Enter a sales conversation–some of your high-priced programs or one-to-one services require a sales conversation before the person will be ready to buy.
- Click to indicate who they are and what they are looking for–this is market research, and in some cases you might not have anything for sale but are instead gathering information.
- Build a long-term relationship with you– you'll want to stand out from the crowd, and you might focus on giving loads of great value.

Step #4: Create the Journey

What kind of experience do you want prospective clients to take? Think again about inviting people into your home and the journey you want them to enjoy.

- Where do they need to start? What do you want them to know? The focus here is on providing really great value at no cost. For example, you might create a free video training series about your area of expertise, or put together an amazing white paper resource for them.

  TIP: If you aren't sure what to give them at the beginning of their journey, try using this strategy that I got from one of my coaches a few years back: Create a list of the Top 10 Questions That People Ask, and one of the Top 10 Questions That People Don't Ask (But Should). This gives you some really great material to work with regardless of how you package it.

- What do you want them to do next? What do you want them to buy? Which of your Anytime Offers is their best starting point? It could be a low-priced item (an online sale) or high-priced item (a sales conversation).

- What do you want them to do if they don't buy? How do you continue the relationship? At the least, they will join your ezine list. You might have a secondary offer available to those who don't take advantage of your first offer.

Tree-Trunk Strategy

I like to look at the journey as a tree trunk.

- Have a main sequence (the tree trunk) that appeals to all your leads. This is your freebie, such as a five-part training series.

- Each goal is a secondary sequence (a tree branch); that is, they click for information on a course and enter that secondary sequence.

131

Tree Trunk Strategy

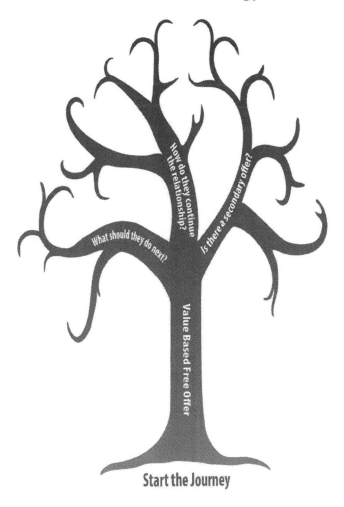

How do they continue the relationship?

Is there a secondary offer?

What should they do next?

Value Based Free Offer

Start the Journey

You can have more than one branch off the tree trunk. If they don't click on secondary sequence #1, you can present another option to them later. The top of tree trunk is your ezine. If someone doesn't take action via the tree trunk, they end up on your ezine for long-term relationship building.

I also recommend keeping the first few emails in your tree trunk heavy on the value/education, and light on the marketing. If you come out of the gate too strong with "buy this!" you will turn people off. If you give them great value in the first few emails, they'll be more open to a later email with an offer to purchase.

Step #5: Create Your Automated Marketing Map

Now that you have all the pieces, it's time to put them together into what we call an *Automated Marketing Map*.

- Map out each step in flow-chart format.

- Aim to have at least three to five emails in each sequence. Keep the focus on providing value, especially for the first few contacts!

Visit the ET Toolbox at the back of the book for a link to download a couple of sample Automated Marketing Maps.

Technology

We like to use, and highly recommend, Infusionsoft for automating your marketing. I've worked with many tools over the years, and this is the best one I've found for automating marketing. Some of the key marketing features (to name a few):

- You can respond to prospects based on their behavior. For example, if someone clicks a link, they get X. But if they don't click a link, they continue to get Y. Most other systems don't allow you to do this.

- You can easily segment your lists and continue to market specifically to people who are only interested in certain things. For example, instead of sending an offer to your entire list, you can send it to people who have NOT bought yet. (One of my biggest pet peeves is when people keep sending me promotions asking me to buy something that I already bought from them— annoying!)

- Your Automated Marketing Map can be created directly in Infusionsoft via their super-cool visual Campaign Builder instead of using a separate flowchart or mind-mapping software.

- Their Opportunity Module is really great for managing the sales process and continuing the conversation.

Regardless of what you choose to use, be sure that it allows you to track and respond to people based on their behavior. And if you want to learn more about Infusionsoft, we have some goodies for you in the ET Toolbox at the back of this book.

Ways to Reach Out (aka Touch People)

It's no longer just about sending emails, Baby! Although emails are still highly effective as part of your follow-up strategy (despite what some might say),if you use a system like Infusionsoft you don't have to use email exclusively. You can also setup automated marketing strategies that include:

- Email
- Phone calls (assigned as a task)
- Voice broadcast

- Fax
- Letter/postcard
- Other goodies such as sending them a CD

Your Automated Marketing Map might be all email or a mix of the above. (For example, email with a voice broadcast and a task assigned to your sales team to make a call.) Below are some ideas for different topics and themes for reaching out to prospects during a sequence. **Remember your goal and take them by the hand on a journey. Focus on building relationships while providing value.**

- Give them proper information right away!

- Ask them a quick question or short survey.

- Give a case study.

- Highlight some key information.

- Invite them to an unadvertised bonus.

- Let them know what's next if they want more.

- Give them a welcome call.

- Give them a coupon or discount for something else.

- Share testimonials and stories.

- Ask for testimonials and stories.

- Invite them to become affiliates.

- Ask if they received X shipment, such as your book.

A Sample Sequence

When people purchase the OBM book:

- Day 0–confirmation email
  "Order confirmed – book is on its way."

- Day 1–quick question email
  "What is your biggest question about X?"

- Day 3–cool story email with comments
  "Loved this story from X, just had to share."

- Day 5–favorite part of book email
  "Have you read page XX yet?"

- Day 10–did you get your book? Email
  "Just want to make sure you received your book."

- Day 15–what is your favorite part of book email
  "Would love to hear from you."

- Day 20–next OBM Training notification
  "If you want more, be sure to sign up for X."

Some final tips:

- When creating your emails and promotional material, write conversationally. You don't have to be a copywriter to do this! That being said, if you aren't a good writer, hiring someone to help you is a REALLY good idea. **Writing the emails is the #1 place where people get stuck in this process.** If you hate writing, hire a copywriter (Use the thirty-day rule —if you can't get it done in thirty days, then you need to hire help.)

TIP: if you don't want to hire a copywriter but struggle with writing, have someone else do a draft that you can edit. I call this the *ping-pong strategy*, and it can be highly effective. For example, Tiffany will write a draft of something for me and send it over to me to edit. In some cases I make a slight tweak, and in other cases I practically rewrite the whole thing! The point is that she got the ball rolling, and once it was rolling I was able to easily edit and finish the writing.

- If you have a lot to offer in your business, focus on making it as simple as possible. It can be tempting to try to squeeze five things into your marketing map, but you might confuse people, and a confused mind doesn't buy. You need to pick your top one or two offers to include in your initial map, and then build other up sells from there as needed.

- Look to add one-to-one contact in more touches rather than fewer! Don't be shy about inviting people to a phone call, especially if you offer a very specialized or high-end program. Some people think that prospects aren't open to a conversation, but I think it's actually the opposite – people are HUNGRY for personal contact and quite often prefer to hop on the phone when they are ready for more information.

My Challenge to You

Get your first sequence setup within thirty days.

Yes, this can feel like a lot of work upfront—and it can be! But keep in mind that long-term payoff and why you are doing this.

137

CHAPTER 10
YOUR TEAM

It's time to dive into the final section of the Automate Your Growth Formula—your team.

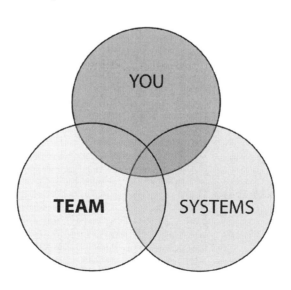

I have a special treat here for you in this section that I'm REALLY excited about and which will give you step-by-step guidance to finding, hiring, and working with the right virtual support team for you. But first I want to set the stage with a short rant.☺

I get annoyed when business owners can't find the help—the right virtual support teams—they need to support them and their growing businesses. It goes without saying that no great thing is accomplished alone, right? We all know that any thriving business needs to have a strong support team in place. And yet many of the entrepreneurs I talk to struggle in this area—everything from outright nightmare stories (people stealing money, running off with lists, or disappearing never to be heard from again), to just plain settling for help that "isn't quite what I need but I don't know how or where to find the help I really need so I'll make do with what I have."

It's actually the second scenario that scares me more—the settling. Nightmare scenarios are pretty straightforward in that they have to be dealt with when they happen. Your virtual assistant has disappeared off the face of the earth and taken all of your information with her... you have no clue how to access your website, login to your shopping cart, or even contact your own clients. When this kind of stuff happens, you are forced to deal with it or your business could literally sink. (TIP: As we've talked about already, having your virtual office setup with everything centralized would prevent this. Be sure you ALWAYS know how to access your stuff.)

I was talking to a business owner the other day who shared with me: "I know my VA isn't the right one for me, but she'll do for now. She's a really great gal, just not the one for me." What scares me more than the nightmare scenario is what I know a number of you are dealing with right now: You have a team in place—a virtual assistant or two, a web designer, marketing support, maybe some associate coaches – but the team isn't truly serving you to the fullest extent possible. You know this, but you don't know what to do about it, how to fix it, or even how it could or should be different, so you ignore it and let things be "good enough."

"Good enough" could be the death of your business, ESPECIALLY when it comes to hiring your virtual team. This is an issue that is near and dear to my heart, and I'll tell you why. My experience has given me the unique perspective of being able to see both sides of the coin. I've been the virtual support professional working for my clients as an Online Business Manager, and I have also been the business owner hiring my own team (and helping other business owners hire theirs, too).

There is nothing I love more in the world than seeing an entrepreneur connect with the right team member for them, and everyone is happy and thriving. When this happens I know that I've made an impact (which is what we all really want to do, right?).

Throwing Spaghetti at the Wall and Hoping Someone Will Stick

With the changes in my own business over the past few years, I've gone from being the support person to being the entrepreneur who is hiring her own support team. As I've shared already, I hired my OBM, Tiffany, and a few VAs during this time, plus I have a whole bunch of really great folks who help me with project-based things like graphic design, web design, creating videos, and such.

So I'm now on the other side, if you will, and I'm experiencing firsthand what it means to have great support in your business (or not). I have the unique perspective of being able to stand in the middle and see what is going on. Now that I've expanded my services to help entrepreneurs find their Online Business Managers and other team members, I've also been talking directly to many of you and hearing your stories—the great, the ick, and the dreaded "good enough."

Here is a common scenario I see when it comes to hiring:

The entrepreneur has a business and knows they need some stuff done (like setting up a website and shopping cart), so they ask around and find out that they need to hire a virtual assistant. Great! But where to find one? So their friend says, "I know so-and-so works with Suzy, why not contact her?" So you call Suzy, have a great conversation, and hire her on the spot... and then nothing happens."I've hired Suzy, why isn't my business now skyrocketing? She must not be very good. I need to find someone else." So you fire Suzy and post your opportunity at a VA directory site and get twenty responses. Eek! How do you sort through them to find the one who is the best fit for your business? You setup calls with a few of them, and Harriet says she can take care of those things for you. She comes on board and blasts out of the gate getting stuff done left, right, and center. She gets your website setup and everything is hunky dory for a few months. But then things start to slow down and she's not doing much for you anymore. What's up? Even though you like Harriet, you aren't sure what else to give her to do. She is so helpful, always asking, "How can I help?" but you just don't know what to give her and things start to fizzle. Once again you are left wondering, "I thought Harriet was perfect here, but now she seems to not be working out." And so you start looking for someone else again...

And so on, and so on...

This is what I call the *throwing spaghetti at the wall and hoping someone will stick* approach to hiring—and I see it WAY too often. Some people do get lucky with this approach and end up with the right person. But more often than not they end up with the wrong person for what they actually need help with.

Nine times out of ten it's not about the person you hired, it's about you. Because you weren't clear on your needs before hiring, you simply ended up hiring the wrong person. Or you hired the right person but didn't know what to do with them. Maybe you hired someone for the wrongs reasons, such as liking them as a person, rather than for what they could do for your business.

There are definitely some duds out there. **However, as a business owner I believe WE need to take complete responsibility for our teams and, therefore, the success of our businesses.** No more blaming someone else when things fall apart—we need to make a decision to own it and fix it ourselves.

I was talking to a colleague of mine who has had her share of team headaches over the years. This woman has created a truly thriving business that hit seven figures last year and is poised to multiply that this year and beyond. She is successful, and yet within all this success her team was bringing her and her business down. This had been happening for years, including nightmare stories from her past (stolen lists) to her current team which is borderline

143

"good enough"—and things started to get nasty. (Funny thing about "good enough" is that it doesn't stay good for long... things either get better or they fall apart.) She is a pretty enlightened gal, and she could see how her own behavior had allowed some of the problems to continue. She made the decision to face the issue head on, and talked to her team about how she hasn't been the best leader she could have been and how things are going to change. And a funny thing started to happen: The people who are good fits and truly want to support her thriving business stepped up. And those who weren't ready for that simply fell away so she could hire the right people instead.

Many entrepreneurs don't have hiring experience. They know they need a team to support the growth of their business, but they have no clue who to hire, where to find them, or how to work with them once they are hired. **Unfortunately, we don't have a human resources department to take care of this for us, so the responsibility falls on our plate,** and we default to throwing spaghetti at the wall and crossing our fingers that someone will stick!

We are so afraid of hiring – afraid of not finding the right person, afraid of hiring the wrong person, afraid of wasting a bunch of money and then having to hire all over again—that we just jump at the first person who pops up and say to ourselves, "Thank goodness! I'll just hire this person then I don't have to deal with this anymore."

We hire because we want relief; because we are afraid and not quite sure how to build a team. And when you hire on that kind of weak foundation, it's almost a guarantee that things will fall apart.

It's time for us to step up and take responsibility for two things:

1. Getting super clear on our needs so we can find and hire the right virtual support professionals for our team (and put down the spaghetti).

2. Ensuring we create a strong and thriving working relationship with everyone on the team.

TIP: There are two questions you need to answer before you hire:

At what stage is your business? There are three key stages to business growth as it applies to hiring the right virtual team. You need to hire different team members at each stage. If you try to run a seven-figure growing business with a start-up team, there will be issues.

Where are you headed? Determine what you want to accomplish in the next year or so BEFORE you hire. What revenue streams are you creating? What projects are you working on? What kind of marketing will you be doing? When you are clear on where you are headed, you can find the right people to support you.

Team Success Formula

There is a lovely little recipe for successfully working with your team:

Entrepreneur provides the WHAT
Team provides the HOW
Combine ingredients to create a thriving business.

When it comes to working with your team you need to be able to clearly provide the WHAT to them—what is the vision, what is going on in the business, what is coming up, what you want to see accomplished (or don't want to see at all).

It's just that simple!

Remember when we talked earlier about the ostrich and the control freak? This distinction comes into play with your team as well.

The Ostrich

An ostrich hires a team member (or two) and then promptly puts their head in the sand and hopes that their team will get the job done. They don't want to have to deal with their team at all, and have the unrealistic expectation that their team will be able to do their job with little or no input from them as the business owner.

An ostrich expects their team to be able to read their mind and know what it is that needs to be done. They may not think of it this way, but I assure you that this is how their team sees it. And it is HIGHLY frustrating for them as they are left to fend for themselves and try to decipher what is going on and what needs to be done. They either go with what they think is right and do the wrong thing (which is a huge waste of time and money), or they get stuck in non-action because they don't know what to do (so nothing gets done and the ostrich gets frustrated and/or angry).

In my experience, ostriches are generally stuck themselves. They aren't sure WHAT they are doing in their own businesses and hence are unable to provide that information to their teams. Some business owners

146

get so stuck in trying to figure out what to do that they unconsciously try to abdicate the success of their businesses to their teams.""I'll just hire a virtual assistant and they'll tell me what to do and be able to get my business going for me, phew!"But it doesn't work that way, and an ostrich ends up wasting oodles of money, time, and heartache trying to hire from this perspective.

What to do? The best thing an ostrich can do is hire a coach or a mentor to help define what they want to create in their business, and THEN hire the team to help them accomplish that.

As your business grows, there will come a point in time when the day-to-day management of the team starts to distract you from doing the things you need to do in order to grow your business. This is a natural part of growth, and this is when you should hire someone like an Onlinc Business Manager to work with the rest of the team directly and take the day-to-day off your plate. This generally happens when a business reaches the six-figure mark in revenue and is ready to really amp up its growth.

The Control Freak

A control freak hires a team member and then either a) doesn't give them anything to do, or b) gives them work to do but tells them exactly how to do it and watches them like a hawk at every step. They want things done in very specific ways and know the best ways to do them, and anyone who tries to step in will never be able to do as good a job as they can.

A control freak knows they need to hire a team to support them, but struggles to let go of things and trust that the team will get them done. In a lot of cases the control freak has been the only one doing the work in their business to date, so when they bring on a team they find it hard to give them something to do and to let them do it in their own way. As a virtual support professional, trying to get the control freak to let go of things so you can take care of them, and then having them hang over your shoulder at every step, can be exhausting. It is extremely demotivating for the team member, and often leads to resentment and anger.

I have control freak tendencies, so I am intimately familiar with this problem. I fear that if I'm not on top of everything ensuring things are done exactly the right way that it will all fall apart. It's a trust issue. Control freaks sometimes bury themselves in the "how" details in order to avoid doing other things in their business like marketing, sales, strategy, and other growth activities. It's easier to default to the "how" stuff than it is to step up and do the necessary marketing and sales work. The "how" is safe and easy; the rest can be hard and scary.

What to do? The best thing a control freak can do is work with a coach or a mentor to get super clear on WHAT they need to do as the entrepreneur and learn to release everything else to their team.

Work with your team from the middle place –being involved enough to provide clarity and direction (the WHAT), while leaving your team free to do their job in their own way (the HOW). It can be a bit of a journey to learn to stay in the middle, but it's the best place to be if you want the support of a team that can truly help you and your business thrive.

TIP: Daniel Pink's book *Drive* is an awesome resource for understanding what motivates people to do great work and that people need to be given space in order to do so. Time for us control freaks to back off a bit, LOL. We discuss this in detail in the THRIVE Hiring System™.

Are You Being Taken Care Of?

At the end of the day this is all that matters when it comes to whether or not you have the right team for you and your business:

Is your team taking care of you, or are you taking care of them?

The answer to this question is usually a gut feeling. You already know the answer whether you want to admit it or not! And knowing that answer is the key to having a team that will truly help you and your business thrive rather than a team that is just "good enough."

I want to set a very high standard for you: **Everyone** on your team should make you feel like you are being taken care of.

One of the entrepreneurs I helped recently in finding some new team members shared with me that for the first time ever in her business she now has "a team that actually cares as much about my business as I do."

Imagine the power of that for a moment... having someone actually CARE about your business as much as you do. I'm a firm believer that your virtual support team should give you a feeling of confidence that they understand what you want and are making it happen. You should feel that they are on your side and that your business is a priority for them. You should feel that they love what they do and really enjoy supporting the success of you and your business. They should be demonstrating – in every little thing that they do – that they CARE.

It is up to you to ensure that you create such a team. I want this for you... no, I demand it of you! Otherwise, as your business continues to grow it will literally suck the life out of you. Whether you are a control freak trying to do it all on your own or an ostrich with your head in the sand, team issues can literally mean the life or death of your business (and sanity!).

I remember talking to an entrepreneur about the various team woes she has had over the years. She has a highly successful multi-six-figure business, and she said to me, "If I have to deal with one more team issue I'm just going to shut down my business." This breaks my heart and brings tears to my eyes.

I KNOW that there are many awesome virtual support professionals out there chomping at the bit to work with you and create a thriving business. I know these people, and have worked with, trained, and collaborated with literally hundreds of them over the years. Online Business Managers, virtual assistants, web designers, graphic designers, blog designers, social media specialists, copywriters, marketing specialists, writers, editors, event managers, bookkeepers, PR specialists, affiliate managers, launch managers, video production specialists... the list goes on. And what these folks love to do is provide you with the support you need to create the business of your dreams. That is what they enjoy doing and what gives them fulfillment. **In other words, all the work you don't know how to do or hate to do... these folks love! How cool is that?**

I remember when I used to work as a corporate recruiter years ago. I approached every placement with the belief that the perfect person for the job was out there; it was just a matter of finding them and connecting them with the opportunity. **The same thing applies to us as entrepreneurs – our ideal team is out there, we just need to get clear, get connected, and away we go.**

There is no longer any excuse to settle. And if you truly want to create a thriving business, you need to take the bull by the horns and get this team thing figured out once and for all.

Don't let good enough be good enough any longer.

CHAPTER 11
THE THRIVE HIRING SYSTEM™

I sat down to write the chapters about how to know who to hire, where to find them, and how to work together, and then I stopped because I had what I consider to be a BRILLIANT idea. ☺Instead of writing those chapters, I'll give you free access to my THRIVE Hiring System™ Essentials Kit. This includes the complete video training program and the materials that I have available for sale at www.THRIVEHiringSystem.com.

I created this program in 2010, and it is one of the best programs I've ever created. (Not to boast, but I've seen the difference this program can make.) I designed it as a step-by-step guide for entrepreneurs in hiring the right virtual support for their businesses. The THRIVE Hiring System™ Essentials Kit includes the following three modules:

Module #1–Team: Who You Need and When (no more guesswork!)

- The two key people that EVERY business owner needs to have on their team (at the very least)
- What to outsource vs. what to keep for yourself

- The three stages of business growth and who you need to hire at each stage (including organizational charts)

- What attributes to look for when hiring a virtual support professional. (This alone could make or break the success of your team!)

- Exactly who you need to hire for your various revenue streams

- Setting expectations to successfully work with virtual support professionals

Module #2–Hire: Find and Hire the Right People (so you stop wasting time and money)

- How to create a job description that appeals to quality support professionals

- The best places to find people (including the new THRIVE Directory & Job Board!)

- How to short-list and interview your top candidates

- Selecting the best person for the business AND for you

- Compensation options and negotiating rates

- How to hire project-based professionals vs. committed team members

Module #3–Release: Letting Go to Clear Your Plate (delegating the right way)

- Why delegation doesn't work (and what to do instead)
- Setting up a strong communication plan with your team members

- Ensuring that you have measures of success in place

- The "inner game" of learning to trust and let go (which is a challenge for many of us!)

This program provides everything you need to get the right team in place now, and yes... it's free to you as a book-reader bonus. (Can I get an Amen?)

You can claim your free gift at:

www.ThriveHiringSystem.com/bookreaderbonus

And just to be clear, there are no strings attached. This isn't cloaked as a gift and you have to buy something else in order to use it or anything nutty like that. You get 100 percent access to these three training modules just as if you purchased them.

You also get access to the THRIVE Directory & Job Board, which has hundreds of virtual support professionals in various areas of expertise who are ready to do great work. Can I get another Amen?

CHAPTER 12
YOUR NEW DEFINITION OF SUCCESS

"Success is doing what you want to do, when you
want, where you want, with whom you want, as
much as you want."—Anthony Robbins

I can't think of a better quote to sum up this book, as this
is what it's really all about.

- *Success is doing what you want to do*–if your business
  doesn't give you ample opportunity to do the things
  you love, then really, why are you in business?

- ... *when you want*–time is the great equalizer, and you
  are 100 percent in control of how you spend it.

- ...*where you want*–be it working from home or
  otherwise, travel or not, we live in a world that allows
  us this choice.

157

- *...with whom you want*–nothing great is ever accomplished alone, and being an entrepreneur allows you the opportunity to work with some of the coolest people on the planet.

- *...as much as you want* – which brings me back to the original question proposed by this book:

How much do you really need to work in order to be successful?

The answer comes back to what is most important to you—freedom, money, or meaning?

If you are driven by freedom, you may be willing to sacrifice opportunities that could bring you more money, in which case you may find yourself saying no to things in order to protect your freedom.

If you are driven by money, you may be willing to sacrifice more of your freedom (time), in which case you will be fine working long hours and days without a break.

If you are driven by meaning, you may be willing to sacrifice more of your money or freedom to fulfill your purpose in the world.

My hope for you is that you have gained clarity on what you want your business to look like and have some of the foundational tools to make it happen. If you are someone who easily falls prey to the "shoulds" (like me), I hope this book has given you permission to chart your own course, create success on your own terms, and say no to opportunities that don't fit your *why* and yes to those that do, even if everyone around you thinks you "should" do otherwise.

If you have been in The Entrepreneur's Trap for a while now, I hope this book has given you a lifeline for getting out, and that you are feeling better already. I assure you there is light at the end of the tunnel, even if you can't see it.

And most of all, I hope that you have booked yourself a vacation... a 100 percent, unplugged, "no phone, email, or business communication of any kind" vacation. I hope you spend an entire week (or heck, a month!) on a beach relaxing, reading a book, and enjoying time with your loved ones.

Be sure to send me a postcard, OK? I can't wait to hear all about it. And if you feel inspired to do so, be sure to drop me a line about your own journey—I would LOVE to hear from you, whether it's to share an "h-ha" or a celebration, or to ask a question... anything goes. I can be reached via email at tina@tinaforsyth.com (yes, that's my direct address), or you can find me online as well atwww.TinaForsyth.com (all my social media links are there as well).

Big hugs! And lots of love on your journey. ☺

Tina

The ET Toolbox

As promised, I've got lots of extra goodies available to you as a compliment to the book: worksheets, checklists, recommended resources, and such.

Just go to the following link to access the ET Toolbox online:

www.TinaForsyth.com/Toolbox

And enter the password:

freedom

HOW CAN I HELP?

There is nothing I love more than helping busy entrepreneurs stop working so darn hard and get the systems and support they need to have their businesses run without them. Dreamy, right?

My awesome team and I have a variety of ways we can work together, including:

- The Automate Your Growth™ 90-Day Workshop
- The Automate Your Marketing Program
- Infusionsoft Implementation and Optimization
- Virtual Team Recruitment Services
- Online Business Management Training
- One-to-one Coaching and Consulting Packages
- VIP Kickstart Planning Days (for those who like to move fast!)

Visit www.TinaForsyth.com for details or reach us via email at team@tinaforsyth.com.

ABOUT THE AUTHOR

Tina's first foray into the business world was at age eight, when she used her trusty tape recorder to create a radio commercial for her family's rental business. (Funnily enough, they didn't use it.)

Since then she has been a "Jill of all Online Trades," working in everything from marketing to recruiting for businesses big and small. She has helped launch, build, and manage multiplesix-figure-plus businesses since starting her online business adventures in 1999.

Tina is considered a leading authority on leveraging your systems, team, and revenue streams so you can setup your business to run without you (woo hoo!). As the founder of the International Association of Online Business Managers and the creator of the Automate Your Growth™ Formula, she provides training, coaching, and consulting to high-endentrepreneurs who are ready to stop working so darn hard and take their businesses to the next level.

Tina lives in Lethbridge, Alberta, with her husband Dan, daughters Sam and Lexi, noisy cat Shadow, and goofy dog Rocky.

You can reach Tina:

By email: tina@tinaforsyth.com

On Facebook: www.facebook.com/tinaobm

On Twitter: www.twitter.com/tinaforsyth

On LinkedIn: www.linkedin.com/in/tinaforsyth